A Game and a Half

A Game and a Half

AN AUTOBIOGRAPHY
Rob Andrew

Hodder & Stoughton

Acknowledgements

I would like to express my sincere thanks to journalist and broadcaster Chris Rea for his tireless efforts in helping me produce this book in such a short period of time. There have been many long hours of discussion and I am delighted with the final result.

I would also like to thank Mima MacKellar for her unstinting efforts to reproduce at great speed the work prepared by Chris. Also I wish to thank Colin Elsey, David Rogers and Mike Brett for trawling their records to provide us with so many excellent action photographs for the book.

Finally, I want to thank my publisher Roddy Bloomfield for his advice, guidance and patience in helping with the book.

R.A.

Copyright © 1994 Rob Andrew

First published in 1994 by Hodder and Stoughton
A division of Hodder Headline PLC

The right of Rob Andrew to be identified as the author
of this work has been asserted by him in accordance with the
Copyright, Designs and Patents Act 1988.

10 9 8 7 6 5 4 3 2 1

British Library Cataloguing in Publication Data

A CIP record for this title is available from the British Library

ISBN 0 340 62481 7

Typeset by Hewer Text Composition Services, Edinburgh
Printed and bound in Great Britain by
Mackays of Chatham plc, Chatham, Kent

Hodder and Stoughton Ltd
A division of Hodder Headline PLC
338 Euston Road
London NW1 3BH

Contents

Dedication

I do not think my parents, Raymond and Mary, ever thought a sporting career beckoned when I came into this world on 18 February 1963. There were no great sporting heroes or traditions in the Andrew background, but I was soon to drive my mother to distraction with untold damage to the flower beds and window panes caused by either a football or cricket ball. My father was always lamenting the state of Yorkshire and England cricket. Has anything changed?

Like all doting parents, they would spend hours as a taxi service ferrying me and my brother Richard to and from primary school matches and village cricket matches. The first rugby matches followed at the age of eleven at Barnard Castle School.

By now the family had been extended by two, my sister Jayne, who is six years younger but happens to share the same birthday, and younger brother David, who has captained the Yorkshire Under 21 rugby side. We have all had a love of sports and continue to participate and follow each other's progress. I would like to thank my parents for the patience and support they have given me over the years, never overbearing but constantly concerned. My brothers and sister have, like all siblings, helped me keep my feet firmly on the ground when things have been going well, and have been there to encourage whenever support has been needed.

Since 1985 when we met and throughout our married life, my wife, Sara, has been at my side through the good times as well as the bad. As with many sporting spouses, I suspect, she has often suffered in silence but has always been there when I have needed a quiet word to boost confidence. Our daughter, Emily, was born in 1990 and, as many of our friends will testify, both deserve a medal for putting up with me. I will always be grateful to them for their support.

There are too many colleagues to mention by name at my employer, DTZ Debenham Thorpe, but I thank them and all those who have worked with me in the company for their time and support since 1986.

Also since 1985, the long suffering England rugby supporters will have seen a good many changes. I thank all those who have supported me during my England career, whether close friends or distant strangers, with kind letters or words, and all those England fans who have now helped turn Twickenham into something of an English fortress. Long may it continue.

CHAPTER 1

Half-Break

A sense of perspective. After a decade of high-level rugby, I'm convinced that this is the secret to long and contented survival in the often neurotic and obsessive world of sport, a world where wide-eyed innocence coexists with ruthless ambition, where gurus are gods and where the gods are frequently petitioned to be gurus. It was in the search for perspective that I landed up in Australia, pushing a car across Sydney Harbour Bridge on Anzac Day in 1986. But the search was likely to be a long one for a perplexed young man who, without warning, had arrived at a crossroads in his career.

I had enjoyed a blissful upbringing on the family farm in Yorkshire with the priceless advantages of freedom and space to indulge in the usual boyhood fantasies of Wembley cup finals and test matches at Lords. On each momentous occasion the opposition was provided by my younger brother Richard who was forced to spend hour after tortured hour keeping goal or toiling in the outfield. Like all healthy fantasies, there was no place for disappointment, no thought of failure. But for me, the fantasy became reality. By the age of twenty-two and with no glittering sporting achievements at school, I had performed in the theatres of my dreams, at Twickenham and Lords; I had won five Cambridge blues, three at rugby, two at cricket; I had captained a side against Allan Border's Australians and had stood up to the grim ferocity of the West Indian pace attack. Little wonder that the press had nicknamed me 'Golden Bollocks', but how was I to know then that, in the fickle world of the media, gold could so quickly turn to clay?

In the mid eighties, selection for England was the modern equivalent of being named as accredited food taster to Attila the Hun. Stability was not a word readily associated with a process which had long since

1

entered the realms of farce. In the twelve months between January 1984 and the beginning of 1985, the selectors had awarded first caps to no fewer than twenty-three players, and when I made my début against Romania in January 1985, I was one of five new caps.

There were nine changes in all from the side which had lost 19-3 to the all-conquering Wallabies. The man I replaced was Stuart Barnes, a decision which triggered an interminable sequence of lively and, at times, heated debate. It has filled countless column inches over the years and has supplied the scribes with reams of material, but a glance at the record books reveals the true extent of what has been a crushingly one-sided contest.

The size and manner of England's defeat by the Wallabies meant that changes were inevitable, and I knew that I was in with a chance of selection. I had put up a strong case. The North's impressive win against the Romanians had given me the opportunity to show what I could do in treacherous conditions, but it was the Varsity Match which, more than anything else, helped to launch my international career. There are days when everything goes wrong and, much less frequently, there are days when everything goes right. Tuesday, 11 December 1984 most definitely fell into the latter category. That day Cambridge produced one of the most irresistible displays in the history of the fixture. The margin of victory, 32-6, was the biggest for fifty-nine years. It was the Light Blues' fifth consecutive win and we scored six tries, three of them in the first twenty minutes. I cannot recall playing behind a pack which won as much loose ball as the Cambridge forwards did during that opening quarter. It is on such occasions, with the luxury of unlimited supply, that one can afford to make outrageous demands. I fielded Hugo MacNeill's kick close to our twenty-two and, in line with our policy that season, although not with this particular game plan, I looked to run rather than to kick. The gaps opened up, Mark Bailey burst down the touchline and Kevin Simms, coming up on the inside, took the scoring pass. Bailey, the captain, whose penetrating intellect had devised the brilliantly original strategy of keeping the game tight for the first twenty minutes, just shook his head. On the day he was happy enough to concede to the precocity of his fly half.

The selection of England's fly half always was, and seems destined always to be, a topic of passionate argument, but as a result of my performance in the build-up to the Romanian game, I was now, at least, the media's choice. I went home for Christmas determined to give body and mind a break from rugby. New Year's Day brought the usual round of social engagements, with a family gathering in the evening. We were on the point of setting off when the phone rang. It was Rory Underwood's mother, Anne. 'Fantastic news – Rob's been picked for England!' Dear Anne, she could not have been more thrilled had it been one of her own. It had, of course, been one of her own the previous season when Rory won his first cap against Ireland. We took our coats off, phoned our hosts to say we'd been delayed and waited for the nine o'clock news. Sure enough, I was in the side to play against Romania. Never had a New Year been so joyously celebrated. I had been selected along with my Cambridge colleagues, Kevin Simms and Simon Smith, both new caps. There was also the reassuring presence of Rory on the wing. We had been team-mates since the age of eleven when we first played together at Barnard Castle School. Our companionship and mutual respect have been forged and strengthened by our rugby experiences with Middlesbrough, Yorkshire, the North, England and the Lions. His is a friendship I prize above all others, and is one which has survived the vicissitudes of top-class sport.

I had never subscribed to the view that Cambridge had modelled their play on the touring Australians. It was an assessment which failed to take account of our exploitation of running rugby in previous seasons, long before the Wallabies arrived. To a large extent, it was a style imposed upon us by the physical limitations of our forwards, but that season the Cambridge side was blessed with an unusually high number of superbly gifted backs, so it made sense to use them. It also seemed sensible to continue that policy at international level. In England's pre-match training I had been greatly encouraged by the attitude of Brian Ashton who was Dick Greenwood's coaching assistant in charge of the backs. There was a refreshing freedom of movement in his training routines with the onus on the individual to make decisions for himself. I felt that tactical judgement, rather than pace and flair, was my chief strength. I also believed that the Romanians, in cricketing parlance, were a side packed with seamers, predictable but damnably difficult to score against. A bit of imagination and inspiration – that was what we needed. As it turned out, what I needed, and what I received, was a bit of divine intervention.

My international career was barely a second old when I had the ball in my hands. Should I kick or should I pass? What would I have done at Cambridge? These were the questions flooding through my distracted mind. I looked to the left and there was Kevin Simms. It had worked in the Varsity Match, so why not now? I took off from our twenty-two and Simms, with the same look of baffled incomprehension that Stan Laurel gave Oliver Hardy, dutifully followed. But the waves which had parted against Oxford came crashing in. There was nothing for it but to pass, and what a stinker it was! A good bloke, Kevin, still only nineteen, but thanks to me, he was about to be beaten to a pulp. Time to offer up a silent prayer. The crowd roared. I looked up, and to my astonishment, saw Rory haring down the wing. Simms, with sublime touch and timing, had somehow got the ball away before the Romanians could reach him. A line-out won by England, and from Richard Harding's pass I dropped a goal. It had seemed like a lifetime, but from first to last it had taken precisely forty-seven seconds. An easy game, this international rugby!

Although I scored eighteen points and England won 22-15, it was an unsatisfactory team performance and one which was ungraciously received by the crowd. They had expected a more adventurous approach, but our forwards were seldom able to establish enough control to allow us to play an expansive game. We did at least succeed in scoring a try, which was more than England had done in their five previous matches. But the critics were unimpressed. They had forecast that there would be a blanket finish for the wooden spoon between the home countries in the Five Nations Championship. France were the overwhelming favourites to win, but once again, the biggest obstacle in their path was likely to be the French themselves. They certainly fell foul of the Irish referee David Burnett in the opening match of their campaign which, because the scheduled fixtures had been disrupted by the bad weather, was against England at Twickenham. This time I kicked all England's points, with a drop goal and two penalties, the second, in the last minute and from fifty yards, to draw the match. Here again, indiscipline cost France ten metres and brought their goal posts into range. But the turning point had come in the first half when Patrick Estève, the French wing, was tackled over our line by Richard Harding, and dropped the ball. A try then, and the French might have been unstoppable.

Two games without defeat constituted something of a record for

England in those days. Welcome as it was, it was clear that even this small success could not be sustained. A total of fifty players had been capped in a year, and a win and a draw was hardly enough to transform habitual losers into regular winners. It was an ailing team operating in a flawed system, and although the selectors' intentions may have been sincere enough, some of their actions were as infuriatingly inconsistent as the performance of the players. England finished with three points that season from a victory over Scotland and defeats by Ireland and Wales. The defeat in Cardiff had, unquestionably, been our worst display in the championship, which made the events at Twickenham the following season doubly satisfying. Despite England's indifferent showing in 1985, I was still treading on air and, so far as the media were concerned, walking on water. They had swept me up to the top of the hill, and I had no reason to believe that they were going to frogmarch me down to the bottom with the same indecent haste. Certainly not after scoring all England's points against Wales in the 1986 match at Twickenham. As against France the previous season, my final kick had been in the closing stages, but on this occasion it was a drop goal in the third minute of injury time, and not merely to draw the match, but to win it.

The truth is that our margin of victory should have been bigger than 21-18. That Wales kept it so close was a tribute to their defensive grit and individual skill, but England's forwards were in commanding form, particularly in the line-out. For me, the joy of seeing that drop goal go over was almost as great as the relief at being selected to play in the match. I had been through a patch of wretched form, so miserable in fact that the selectors had seriously considered leaving me out. But now the full might of the media machinery went into overdrive, and overkill. There was no limit to their prurience. Seventy-one points in six internationals, and in the sports columns were seventy-one things you didn't know about Rob Andrew. Quite a few of them I didn't know myself, but it was all hugely enjoyable, and flattering. The day after the Welsh match I went up to Manchester for *A Question of Sport* and on the Monday I was back in London as a guest on *Wogan*, along with Gareth Edwards. I think that I must have been a bit of an afterthought, but Terry went to great lengths to put me at my ease. The main topics of conversation were violence and the inflated importance of penalty goals. *Plus ça change*. A national celebrity at twenty-two. I kept telling myself that it couldn't last, but perhaps the dream would continue for just a little longer. My reverie was interrupted by the telephone. 'Is that Rob Andrew? Alan Jones here . . . '

I first met Alan Jones during the Wallabies tour the previous season. His already formidable reputation as a coach had been cemented by the exhilarating style of the 1984 Australians, who had beaten all four home countries to achieve their first ever Grand Slam. I had played reasonably well for the North against the tourists, and after the match had been able to have a brief chat with him. It had, perforce, to be brief because, as one of the most charismatic personalities in world rugby, Jones was much in demand. But I wanted to know more about the man and to learn from him. After the tour, Jones stayed on in England. It was then that I got a call from Ian Robertson, the BBC's rugby correspondent, who had been coaching at Cambridge. Robertson had been instrumental in raising the standards of rugby at Cambridge, not only in his role as advisory coach but by encouraging so many promising young players to go up to the University. Its effect on the academic standards of the establishment was another matter! Robertson had rung to invite me to lunch with Alan Jones and John Rutherford, the Scotland and British Lions fly half. Jones had wanted to meet both of us and, I subsequently learned, had paid for Rutherford's fare from Scotland. We lunched at the Sheraton, and for that entire encounter I was transported into a different world. We talked only of rugby – of angles of running, of alignment, of moves and of kicking. I realised then how little I knew and how much there was still to learn.

Even in that short time, I could see that Jones was a man of extraordinary force and intellect. He was consumed by the desire to succeed at whatever he did, be it as a politician, a radio chat-show host or a rugby coach. It was impossible not to be infected by his enthusiasm. He was a dominating if not a domineering character, who was to have a profound influence on my rugby future. For the present, however, he was twelve thousand miles away on the other end of a telephone line, presumably about to offer me his congratulations on my performance against Wales. But Jones never did the obvious. 'How do you fancy playing some rugby in Australia at the end of your season?' I fancied it quite a lot. I knew that I had much to learn and that I had to improve my game if I was to advance my rugby career. There was a self-confidence and a swagger about the Australians that

I secretly admired. I am not, by nature, an overtly confident person, but I recognised that a touch of arrogance was an essential component in a player's make-up, especially in my position, at fly half. I could kick a few goals, I could tackle and I could pass, but my success thus far had come mostly through sheer bloody hard work.

Jones explained the offer in detail. I would go to Sydney at the end of the domestic season in April and play for the first division side Gordon. It was tempting but there were a number of factors to be considered. I had been asked to play for the Yorkshire 2nd XI on a match-by-match basis during that summer, and despite my rapid elevation to international status in rugby, I still harboured a wish to play first-class cricket. If I went to Australia, it would scupper once and for all any hopes I had of making the grade at cricket. It was not an easy decision but one that was made quickly enough. With me in the Yorkshire side at that time were players like Ashley Metcalfe and Richard Blakey. They were talented cricketers, much better than I was, and in my heart of hearts I knew that I wasn't good enough. Nor did I want to totally commit myself to a professional sport and have to sever my links with rugby. The days when the gifted all-rounder could play both sports at the highest levels were long gone.

There was also my career to think about. I had come down from Cambridge the previous summer and had taken up a post as a trainee chartered surveyor with a company in Nottingham. While I was there, I was offered a position in London with Debenham, Tewson and Chinnocks, who had offices all over the world including, by happy chance, Sydney. I had already agreed to join them in the autumn, but if I could somehow make a little bit of money from business while I was in Australia, it would add immeasurably to my pleasure. They agreed that I could join them six months early, and that I would start in the Sydney office at the beginning of May. All that remained was for me to break the news to my girlfriend, Sara.

Sara and I met through rugby. She was studying pharmacy at Nottingham University when I was at Cambridge, and it was after a club match against Nottingham that we were introduced by Brian Moore. Perversely, at the same time as I left Cambridge to move to Nottingham, Sara moved from Nottingham to Cambridge, but our relationship survived. Indeed it flourished. I would miss her a lot. Sara left me in no doubt about her feelings on the subject, but after innumerable and costly candlelight suppers, and the promise of a three-week holiday in Australia, I eventually talked her round. If I did have any lingering doubts about the wisdom of the trip, they were soon dispelled.

The newspapers carrying the glowing reports of my *tour de force* against Wales were barely off the shelves when we travelled to Edinburgh for the Calcutta Cup. I now realise, of course, that yesterday's heroic deeds are tomorrow's statistics, but I was too much of the innocent to understand it then. England were not exactly prepared for what happened at Murrayfield either. We were slaughtered 33-6. To make matters worse, Gavin Hastings had eight kicks at goal and converted the lot, while I missed five out of seven. Before the match a newspaper carried a picture of me playing the bagpipes, underneath which was the caption 'Tunes of Glory'. It was mischievously reprinted after the débâcle with the words 'Pipe Dreamer'. If the team got a panning from the press, it was tame in comparison to the venom directed at me. Most hurtful of all was the criticism from John Scott, the former England captain and number eight. He described me as the worst player ever to have represented England. It was an absurd comment, but I was deeply upset by it. If that was what Scott felt – Scott who had himself experienced stinging rebuff as a player – then what must the rugby community at large think? I had accepted the good press, so logic demanded that I must accept the bad.

Criticism about my form was valid. I had lost my edge and some of the *joie de vivre* of my student days when the sole responsibility, it seemed to me, was to have a good time. But now there was a job to protect and a career to pursue. I had become introverted, with the result that the fear of losing was overshadowing the enjoyment of playing. I redeemed some of the lost ground in the next match against Ireland, which we won 25-20 and in which Dean Richards marked his début with two pushover tries. It was a welcome, if temporary, truce in hostilities with the press. But I remained firmly in their sights, and after England's final humiliation of that season, against France in Paris, I was savaged again. Bondi Beach was becoming more appealing by the minute. I knew that my decision to leave England would be misinterpreted in certain quarters. The tabloid dependence on pictures and pulp meant that I was variously depicted as a quitter and a wimp. I was neither, but I needed the break to replenish my fast-draining supplies of confidence, and to take stock.

Sydney was *en fête* for Anzac Day, a public holiday in Australia, and the city sparkled in the early autumn sunshine. Already I felt a sense of well-being. Alan Jones was at the airport to meet me, armed with a hectic schedule of events for the day. Jet lag was not a condition recognised by a man who existed on three hours of sleep and who lived every second of his waking hours to the full. It was pointless to plead travel fatigue. Tomorrow, maybe, I could rest. The first stop was the Gordon Club, where a barbecue was in full swing and where I would meet the club officials and most of my new team-mates. I wondered what their reaction would be to this English intruder. They must have read the press cuttings from the Five Nations Championship, and I hoped to hell that they'd missed the reports of the games against Scotland and France. On the other hand the club badly needed a decent fly half. I had the advantage of knowing a number of players who were already playing with other clubs in Sydney, among them Clive Woodward, the former Leicester and England centre, and Steve Holdstock, my old team-mate at Nottingham. I was quickly warming to the place, the climate, the club and the company.

My fears that I might be seen as a threat by some of the players and as an unwelcome interloper by others quickly evaporated. Their undisguised delight at seeing me did, however, suggest that the team was in dire need of some help. They were not exactly intoxicated by success, suffering more than most from the club system. Despite the fact that all clubs, even those reserve sides in the fifth grade, play in a competitive league structure, the premier competition is the inter-state championship. Very often in the midst of the league season, clubs would have to surrender their best players to the state side (in Gordon's case, New South Wales), and while this was a relatively minor inconvenience for richly endowed clubs like Randwick, it severely disrupted the weaker ones like Gordon. It soon became apparent that Gordon were overdependent on their two Wallaby forwards, Steve Cutler and Mark Harthill. Duncan Hall, who had played for Australia some years earlier but who still represented the state, was another key player. When these three were available, Gordon could compete with the best, but without them, they were no better than a mid-table side. This would be a challenging season, which also coincided with the club's fiftieth anniversary.

The anniversary celebrations had begun on the day of my arrival. Alan Jones, as ever, was the life and soul of the party, although Gordon was not his club. Before his appointment as national coach, he had coached Manly, but he had recommended me to John Fordham, a Gordon official, whose brother Bob had refereed the England v Wales game that season and who was later to become chief executive of the Australian Rugby Union. The Fordhams became good friends and treated me as one of the family during my stay. With incipient jet lag taking its toll, I went in search of Alan Jones. I wanted nothing more than a place to rest my head, 'C'mon,' said Jones, 'we're off to Sydney Cricket Ground.' Good God, had the man signed me up to play cricket as well? 'No, no – it's the big rugby league game.' This was unreal – here I was at Gordon rugby union club, on my way to one of the world's most famous cricket grounds to watch rugby league. If that seemed bizarre, it was nothing to the journey ahead. Halfway across the Harbour Bridge, the car spluttered to a halt. We had run out of petrol in the one place where the penalty for stopping was akin to penal servitude. 'Get out and push,' barked my guide, mentor and, until that moment, friend. In that instant, I would have given a XXXX to be somewhere else. And yet in that situation of toe-curling embarrassment, there was also wonderment. I was in a different world, and after my recent experiences in England, a different world was exactly where I wanted to be.

The Sydney Cricket Ground was all I had imagined it to be, the colonial balustrades of the pavilion through which the genteel giants of cricket had passed now shaking with the weight of those grizzled mastodons of rugby. I marvelled at the speed of the game and winced at its power. It was then that Jones told me that I'd be playing my first game for my new club the next day. And then, as if to soften the blow, 'But don't worry – you'll be turning out for the 5ths.' What I hadn't appreciated was that the 5ths, like the 1sts, played in a competitive league with championship points at stake, and that the next day the entire Gordon club would be playing their archrivals Manly from top to bottom. Our match was due to start at ten in the morning, with the big game between the first teams kicking off at three o'clock. I couldn't believe how seriously the game was taken at the lower levels. Bagford Vipers would have been appalled. The team talk before our game against Manly was as impassioned as any delivered by a captain about to lead his side on to the international field. By the end of the game we had been hammered and I was ready for the knacker's yard. 'Tomorrow's Sunday,' said Jones soothingly.

I was awakened from the deepest sleep I have ever experienced. Alan Jones was framed in the doorway dressed in running kit. 'Thought you looked a bit sluggish yesterday,' he said. 'So this morning we'll do a little bit of running.' I was beginning to have second thoughts about this man. The original intention was that I would find accommodation when I got to Sydney, but until then I would stay with Jones. As things turned out, however, Jones was so seldom at home that it was just as convenient for me to stay there. It was the ideal arrangement, although on that first Sunday morning, I wasn't so sure. After a season of domestic rugby, there was no problem with my general levels of fitness. I had the stamina to survive a hard game, and I knew that I could sustain my sprints over short distances. But what I was not prepared for, and what this devil incarnate forced me through, was a series of power running over distances of 200–400 metres. Never in my life have I experienced such lung-bursting pain. I pleaded, I implored and I beseeched, but Jones was oblivious to my agony.

After such an inauspicious start, it was difficult to know on what evidence the selectors had based their decision to pick me for the first team the following Saturday against Eastern Suburbs. The training sessions before the game were enjoyable and invigorating, with far greater emphasis on speed and ball work. The most marked difference to English training, however, was the intensity of the practice sessions. This was, of course, my introduction to a system where every match was given extra significance by the need to accumulate league points. At home, where ancient tradition, not current strength, determined fixture lists, club organisation was ludicrously haphazard by comparison. The Australian way had to be the example to follow for club sides in England. I was to learn more about the skills and science of rugby in the next few weeks than at any other time in my career, before or since, including the truth behind the myth of Australian back play. The common perception is that Australian sides run the ball from all parts of the field and in almost every situation. The reality is very different. If anything, Australians kick the ball more than we do. Admittedly, they tend to kick more intelligently with a far deeper awareness of reclaiming the ball, and there are more players who can kick accurately and with greater variety than there are in this country. But they do kick a lot.

If I learned one lesson above all others during my spell in Sydney, it was the value of sheer aggression in everything. Australian players will dedicate hours of their practice time to contact work. That is why they are such superb tacklers. I was always confident about my tackling, based on a technique which had been classically taught and carefully supervised at school. You either have the ability to tackle or you don't, and despite popular belief, courage has very little part to play in it. Now I was learning about the other vital ingredient, aggression. Acceleration into the tackle, and how to make every ounce in a paperweight frame count against eighteen stone of teak-hard muscle. The lessons, some of them punishingly hard, were repeated over and over again. The Andrew machine was slowly getting meaner, and I revelled in my new-found strength. I looked forward with eager anticipation to every match, and began to flourish in the competitive environment.

Gordon won the first three games in which I played, the most prized scalp of all being that of Randwick. They were the élite club in the country, the Australian equivalent of Bath. Their team sheet read like a roll call from the hall of fame – Campese, the Ellas and Simon Poidevin, the Australian captain. As a result of their prodigiously gifted players, they had developed a uniquely adventurous style, bordering on the reckless. This always gave less talented, but more determined, opponents a chance. On this occasion, Gordon were able to field a full-strength side and, eyeballs out, we won 31-15. It was an astonishing result, and I basked in its afterglow. Three games, three wins and a personal haul of forty-three points. Not only that, but I had received the ultimate accolade from an opponent who, from contorted lips, spat out the words, 'You Pommie bastard.' No whingeing Pom this. I was enjoying the life and, something I had not thought possible a few weeks before, I had resumed my love affair with rugby.

The victory over Randwick was the first and, in retrospect, one of the last high points of Gordon's season. They finished in mid table, but throughout the season I never lost my enthusiasm for playing. The Australian way of life suited me well. Sporting prowess was admired and my contacts through rugby opened any number of doors. My work was progressing well and my social life was full. John Fordham and his wife, Veronica, had taken me into the family fold, determined that I would never suffer from homesickness. But I was beginning to miss Sara, and waited impatiently for the three weeks we would spend together when she came out to visit me. When she arrived we took to the tourist route in Sydney, went to Canberra and flew to the Blue Mountains. Australians think nothing of flying hundreds of miles just for a bash, and on one occasion we hopped into a plane for a party hosted by friends in the Hunter Valley. Our brief encounter with culture was a visit to *Cats* with the Woodwards and the Holdstocks. It was all too easy to be beguiled by the lifestyle. Sara and I talked increasingly about settling down and making our home in Australia. I even harboured the thought that I might play for the Wallabies. But by the end of Sara's stay we had come to the conclusion that our rosy view of Australian life was inevitably tinged by novelty. Sydney for a break was one thing, Sydney for life might be very different.

I began to dread Sara's departure. I would miss her terribly, and what was more I was beginning to miss England. Alan Jones sensed my mood. He had arranged a dinner for Sara and me on our last evening together. A car came to collect us and took us to the Sheraton Wentworth, one of Sydney's swankiest hotels. There was a reception party to greet us when we arrived, and as we walked into the foyer, the orchestra struck up with music from *Cats*. Jones had planned everything, down to the last detail. It was typical of him. Sensitive, intimidating, compassionate, generous and woundingly critical, he is all of these. He is a man of great complexity, with diverse interests and a brilliant mind. Often, after dinner, we would sit in his kitchen with a bottle of good wine, talking long into the night on a whole range of topics. He has a view, and invariably an extreme one, on everything. No matter what the subject, he approaches it with compelling enthusiasm and passion. I have never met anyone more skilled at firing and motivating an audience. As a speechwriter for former prime minister Malcolm Fraser, he has a deep knowledge and understanding of politics, and even stood as a candidate in the New South Wales state elections. There was talk that he might become prime minister himself, and it wouldn't surprise me if he were to succeed in this quest.

Above all, Jones loved to talk rugby, about players and strategies. He immersed himself in the lives of the players. He knew them and their families. He shared in their joys and sorrows. He helped them with jobs, cars and houses, and, on occasions, lent them money. His loyalty to them was total, but he demanded nothing less in return. He was deeply disappointed when some of them fell short of his expectations, or couldn't live up to his exacting standards. The more intense the relationship, the more bitter and hurtful is the ending of it, and Jones could be very unforgiving to those he believed had let him down. He regarded it almost as a betrayal.

In the Bledisloe Cup series of 1986, the Wallabies had beaten the All Blacks in the first test, but had lost the second. Jones had been publicly critical of a few of his leading players, notably Simon Poidevin, Nick Farr-Jones and David Campese, whom he had lyrically described to the press before the match as 'the Bradman of rugby'. In the build-up to the third and final test, Jones worked the Australian squad as they had never been worked before. The sessions were superb examples of efficiency and precision, at the end of which the players could hardly drag their bruised limbs off the field. The Wallabies won 22-9, and I went into their changing room at the end of the game. There was the usual heady concoction of alcohol and emotion – champagne, tears, beer and tomfoolery. But, above all, there was the sweet, sweet smell of success. That day the Wallabies knew they were the best in the world. It was not a fleeting fantasy, it was fact. And after six months in Australia I now had some idea of how it had been achieved. More than anything else, I wanted that success for England.

CHAPTER 2

Down Under Again

I returned home from Australia mentally refreshed and physically stronger. I was undoubtedly more confident and with a harder competitive edge. Alan Jones had played a prominent part in my rehabilitation. 'Confidence,' he had said, 'comes from technique. If you miss touch it's a technical problem. If you keep missing touch that technical problem begins to affect your confidence. Get the technique right and the confidence will automatically return.' But if I was a better and more complete player, I couldn't help thinking that the bittersweet experience of the past year had changed me as a person. The sustained assault by certain sections of the media, and the vitriolic nature of some of the criticism, had hit their mark. During that most unpleasant period in my career I did, as I was to do so often in the future, offload some of my emotional baggage on to Sara. Throughout our years together, she has been the wisest of counsellors and staunchest of supporters, but, at that early stage in our relationship, she must have wondered just what it was she was getting into.

I had been surprised by the unhelpful attitude of the team management during these periods of personal turmoil, although in retrospect it was perhaps naive of me to expect sympathy. The selectors have a hard enough job as it is without wet-nursing everyone who falls prey to media attack or who loses form. It is, however, a traumatic time for players who, in most cases, are simply not equipped to deal with it, and a little understanding might help to cushion the shock. But the worst, I hoped, was over. The new season offered fresh hope and exciting challenges.

Deep in the prehistoric forests of the game's administration, a mighty beast was stirring. Friend or foe, no one could be quite certain at this stage. There have always been those flat-earthists who believed that sex would never catch on or that television had no future, and now there were a number of rugby mandarins telling us that there was no demand for a World Cup. In hindsight, it is easy to sneer but, as I recall, there was no great enthusiasm for the venture from the British players, whose competitive needs at international level were catered for by the Five Nations Championship. The impetus for the World Cup had come from the southern hemisphere, where there was an ever-increasing risk of isolation and an ever-growing threat from rugby league.

As the originators of the plan, it was only proper that the inaugural tournament should be held in the Antipodes, although the wisdom of playing the competition in two countries, Australia and New Zealand, was highly questionable. Short of a calamity, England could at least expect to reach the quarter-finals, although the draw had not been especially kind to us. Japan and the United States would be easy hurdles, but Australia, the other country in our pool, were strongly fancied to win the tournament.

Furthermore, England would have to play all their pool matches in Australia, a country singularly ill equipped to stage an event of this size and complexity. Rugby union, despite the higher profile it was getting as a result of the standards set by the international side, remained a distant third in popular appeal behind the league code and Rules football. In truth, the competition was disappointingly low-key on both sides of the Tasman Sea, but especially so in Sydney where the Concord Oval was far from ideal as a rugby venue. So lamentable was the marketing and promotion of the whole operation that the level of public interest in Australia was even lower than we had expected.

What I had learned from my sojourn down under the previous season was that the All Blacks and the Wallabies would be better prepared both mentally and physically than players from the home countries. The fitness levels of the two were almost beyond comparison. It was always a source of amusement, bordering on wonderment, to Tom McNab, who was to play such an important part in changing attitudes to fitness in this country, that some of England's top rugby players were also internationally renowned drinkers. In the early part of my international career, some of the wildest nights were held not on a Saturday, after the match, but on the Friday before it. No longer is that the case, and McNab can take some of the credit.

A rare bird was McNab. It is pretty much a precondition of the best raconteurs that they are also the most enthusiastic *bon viveurs* but, despite the fact that McNab could talk the hind legs off a donkey, and was a thoroughly agreeable companion, the ultimate virtue for him was having a healthy mind in a super-fit body. Secretly, I think, he admired those players who could train flat out, drink themselves to the point of oblivion afterwards and then turn up on time and as fit as fleas for training the following morning. But it was not his idea of how to train athletes for top-class competition.

Above all, McNab was passionate about his sport and the single-minded pursuit of excellence. Among his protégés was Daley Thompson, and later that season Marcus Rose, Kevin Simms and I frequently met up with Thompson at the Haringey Stadium where we went to train under McNab's guidance. I don't think that Thompson was any more impressed by the dedication and devotion of rugby players to their sport than McNab but he, too, derived some perverse enjoyment from our efforts.

McNab was present at our first squad session of the 1986–87 season, held at Loughborough University. So was Judy Oakes, the women's national shot-putt champion, who, to the huge embarrassment of the forwards, outlasted every one of them on the bench presses. McNab despaired of me as an athlete. Unlike Rory Underwood who, with the proper guidance and attitude, could have become a world-class athlete, I was in the egg and spoon class. I can still hear McNab's plaintive cries, 'For Christ's sake, Rob, jelly jaw, jelly jaw!' Jelly jaw was one of the Scotsman's favourite phrases, designed to keep sprinters relaxed when they were running. 'The key to top-class sprinting is relaxation,' McNab told us. 'Keep all your muscles relaxed and just imagine that your jaw is made of jelly.' We also had to imagine that we were holding a potato crisp between thumb and forefinger. Crisps and jelly were more in line with what many of us considered to be an acceptable form of training, but gradually, during that season and beyond, by the sheer force of his personality and through the visible improvement in our fitness levels, McNab began to get his message across. Even hardened cynics like Paul Rendall and Gareth Chilcott, for whom yogic flying would have been a more realistic prospect than mastering plyometric drills, were eventually won round.

It was during one of McNab's sessions that we became fully conscious of the intense personal rivalry between Graham Dawe and

Brian Moore. Both hookers were new to the squad, having replaced Steve Brain and Andy Simpson from the previous season. Both were ferociously competitive. We were jogging round the gym, loosening off muscles, with Dawe and Moore in the lead. But this wasn't jogging, dammit, this was running. The pace steadily increased as the hookers were drawn into their own private duel. Totally oblivious to the fact that the rest of us had stopped and were cheering them on in what was a plausible re-enactment of the quadrangle scene in *Chariots of Fire*, the two continued their race. Such passion, such fanatical pride, were the very qualities that England would need in the months and years ahead.

At least this attention to fitness was a start in the herculean task of catching up with New Zealand and Australia. I was disappointed that the England selectors hadn't made more use of my inside knowledge of the Australian game and of my detailed information about the players we would be facing in nine months' time. Mike Weston was chairman of selectors, and Martin Green, the former Cambridge blue, and Moseley back-row forward, was coach. Both were decent, honourably intentioned men. Both had a vision of what they wanted, but neither was able to translate that vision into substance. There were many reasons for this, some of them beyond their control. Although the Divisional Championship had been reintroduced, there was no formally established league structure. The identification of players therefore remained an almost insurmountable problem in a country as large and well stocked with talent as England. Moreover, Weston and Green were as uncertain about their own positions within the national set-up as the players, which made it extremely difficult to formulate a consistent selection policy or a coherent playing strategy.

The selectors' first job that season was to pick an England XV to play Japan, one of our pool opponents in the World Cup. No caps were to be awarded, and the fact that Stuart Barnes had been selected at fly half didn't worry me unduly. It was clear from their selection that they had no idea at this stage about their best combination. But there was nothing to be gained from playing against Japan that autumn, a game England won at a canter. Much more important to my mind was the Divisional Championship in December, which the North, for whom I was playing, won with a storming final performance against London at Sudbury. In the game against a disorganised and largely disinterested South-West side, I had once again outplayed Barnes. It wasn't enough to lift me into the senior team for the national trial but, here again, although The Rest lost 10-9, I felt that I had given the more convincing performance.

When the team was announced to play Scotland in the opening match of the 1987 International Championship, I was back, but not as first-choice goal-kicker. Marcus Rose, who had been picked at full back, was given that responsibility and this was fine by me. For the second year in succession, the weather conspired against us. The Scottish game was postponed and our first opponents were Ireland at Lansdowne Road. It was a game worthy of mention only for the fact that it taught me the harshest of lessons. England were behind 6-0 but still very much in the game when we were awarded a penalty in our twenty-two. I went for touch but missed. Hugo MacNeill, who had fielded the ball, returned a high hanging kick on to our line. Panic. The ball went loose, Ireland scored and England were on their way to defeat. Little things can mean a lot at this level.

Looking back on what was one of the most miserably unfulfilling seasons in England's history, it is interesting to note how many players in the squad were to form the nucleus of the 1991 World Cup side. England were on the right lines, no doubt about that, but the players lacked conviction. There was no real direction, and whilst we may all have felt at the time that we knew where we were going and what we were trying to achieve, it is very clear now that we hadn't a clue. There was hope, of course, but no genuine expectation of success. The target was not to win the World Cup, simply to avoid humiliation. But never mind the World Cup, we were facing humiliation in the Five Nations Championship. A marginally better performance against France than we had managed in Dublin nevertheless produced another defeat, which meant that we were still without a win going into our third match, against Wales in Cardiff where England hadn't won for twenty-four years.

Nineteen sixty-three was a millstone round our necks. This was true for both sides. With every passing year, the pressure grew on Wales to extend their unbeaten run and on England to break the melancholy sequence of defeat. The problem for the Welsh was that they were in decline, a pale shadow of those great sides which had lorded it over the rest of Europe for a decade and more. They were now vulnerable on the ground where previously they had been impregnable. If England's national side wasn't yet strong enough to topple them, there had been clear evidence that the gap between the two countries was closing fast at club level, where Gloucester, Bristol and, in particular, Bath were more regularly enjoying success against the top Welsh clubs.

Richard Hill, the Bath scrum half and England's captain that fateful day in Cardiff, was particularly fired by the prospect of beating Wales, and delivered an impassioned team talk before the game. This, as it turned out, was one of the problems. Too many club scores to be settled in the furnace of the international arena, and no one suffered more from the afternoon's events than Hill himself. England were billeted, as was the custom in those days, at Chepstow, as near to English soil as it was possible to get west of the Severn Bridge. The idea was that we would be cocooned from the claustrophobic hostility of Cardiff during our preparations for the game. But it was merely postponing the inevitable. Sooner or later we would have to emerge from our splendid isolation and come out into the real world, no matter how unpleasant. The atmosphere going into the ground was heavy with menace. There were other more tangible signs of the crowd's intolerance. Wade Dooley had a pint of beer thrown over him as he walked out to inspect the pitch before the game. Other England players were spat at.

It was into this combustible atmosphere that both sides entered, Wales grimly determined to hold on to their past, England equally determined to break with theirs. The game will be remembered for the intemperance of both sides but one in which England, by implication, were deemed to be the transgressors. Neither country, however, emerged with any credit. Of rugby there was precious little. The only light relief was provided by Marcus Rose who, during the course of the game, had coins thrown at him by the crowd. Had that happened at a football match, play would have been suspended until the offenders were removed, but not at the National Stadium, where it was commonplace. Rose, displaying phlegm and dignity in equal measure, collected the money – about £3.50 in total – and handed it to the referee. 'Keep it for me, ref, it's my match fee.'

Standing so far removed from the maelstrom of the forward exchanges, it was impossible for me to see who had hit whom and why, but the story we got afterwards was that Dooley had punched Phil Davies in response to the Welshman's assault on John Hall. Davies left the field with a fractured cheekbone. At the end of the game we trudged off, beaten again and, in the eyes of our own Union, disgraced. Dooley, Chilcott, Dawe and Hill were all suspended for the final match against Scotland and, subsequently, Hill was stripped of the captaincy.

The day that happened was, as Hill recalls, simultaneously the worst and the best of his life. News of his demotion came at the same time as the birth of his first child. It's not easy to find a card with messages of congratulations and commiseration, so I made one up and sent it to him. Hill and I never enjoyed what could be termed a close relationship during our spells in harness as England's half backs. He was too firmly in the Stuart Barnes camp to stand up and be counted as one of my supporters, but I enjoyed playing with him for all that, especially during his second coming in the national side. But he was too fiery a character and perhaps too immature to have been burdened with the captaincy at that stage in his career. When the spark hit the tinderbox in Cardiff, not only was he powerless to prevent it, he may even have assisted in fanning the flames.

Nevertheless, we all felt that the punishments decreed by the Rugby Football Union were ludicrously harsh and wholly disproportionate to the seriousness of the crimes. To make matters worse not one Welsh player was publicly rebuked, let alone banished. As far as I was concerned, it was a case of 'You've got your troubles, I've got mine.' For the first time in my international career – although not, unhappily, for the last in the aftermath of a defeat in Cardiff – I was dropped. With the four players in exile, there were six changes in the side to play Scotland, hardly the best preparation for the World Cup which was, by now, just a couple of months away. The other player to be dropped was the unfortunate Kevin Simms who had come off the mud-caked pitch at the National Stadium with spotless kit. He had touched the ball only once throughout the afternoon, and yet he was again suffering the indignity of losing his place. It was the fourth time he had been dropped in two and a half years, and he was still only twenty-one. Yet England wondered why so few of their most promising young talents ever reached their full potential.

Of more pressing concern to England's players, and the forwards especially, was the inhibiting effect the punishments, post-Cardiff, might have on them. A certain degree of physical robustness is essential for survival at international level, but fears were being expressed by a number of the pack that they would be going into future games severely handicapped by the censorious attitude of the

RFU. The disagreeable aftertaste of that match lingered for at least a couple of seasons.

Three defeats in our three championship games, and only a Scottish side going for the Triple Crown, albeit at Twickenham, where they had won just twice since the War, stood between us and a whitewash. My own confidence, which, barely a few weeks before, had been brimming, was once again shot to pieces. Stuart Barnes, miffed at being left out of the side to play Wales, had withdrawn himself from the bench in Cardiff. He paid dearly for his fit of pique, because Peter Williams, the Orrell fly half who had replaced him on the bench against Wales, now came into the side for the Calcutta Cup. I had moved on to the bench, but had Barnes not been sulking in his tent, I might easily have dropped to number three in the rankings. I might also have missed out on the trip to Australia. But for Barnes's impulsive act in Cardiff, the future could have been very different for both of us.

The victory over Scotland, 21-12, confirmed my view that I would be going to Australia as England's number two fly half. It was a depressing prospect because, unlike a tour, where the majority of players could reasonably expect ot play at least once a week, the World Cup afforded little opportunity for frequent changes in playing personnel. Once England had decided on their best XV, that would be it. I might, with luck, get the chance to play one game against either Japan or the United States. For the rest of the time it would be a case of repetitive stress syndrome, training every day, often twice a day, with the team, yet detached from it. Still, I kept telling myself that there were thousands of players in England who would happily trade places with me. It was after all a privilege to be picked, and the opportunity of being part of the World Cup scene might not come again.

For the first time that season I began to relax and played easily my best game for a very long time, for Yorkshire, in the County Championship final against Middlesex. I still had some allies, few of them, unfortunately, connected with England. Alan Jones, my mentor in Australia, had been quoted at length in one newspaper saying that not only would I be the first name on his team sheet were he an England selector, but that I would also be captain. During my three seasons in the England squad, I had at no time been asked whether I would be interested in the captaincy, nor had I ever courted it. I had never considered my position to be secure enough. That, of course, was true of most of the squad at the time, but it had never rankled with me that I was not viewed as captaincy material, even though I was by then one of the senior members of the side.

When Richard Hill lost his stripes, Mike Harrison, the Wakefield winger and a colleague of mine in the Yorkshire side, was given the captaincy against Scotland, and for the duration of the World Cup. Harrison possessed no great ability as a tactician but was refreshingly cavalier in his approach and was a popular choice with the players. Yorkshire's adventure against Middlesex was typical of how Harrison saw the game and wanted it to be played. He was also an excellent tourist. But this was to be a tour of duty for which England were ill prepared. The opening game against Australia went very much according to form and very much as England had hoped. We lost, but not badly. It seems incredible, in the light of England's achievements in recent years, that the extent of our ambitions in 1987 was damage limitation.

England, in fact, had played rather well, helped, admittedly, by an uncharacteristically shoddy performance by Australia. The Wallabies were also fortunate to have been awarded a try that was never close to being a score. David Campese failed to get downward pressure on the ball, having lost it in a crunching tackle by Peter Williams, but Keith Lawrence, the New Zealand referee, allowed the try. As detrimental to England's prospects of progress to the later stages of the competition, however, had been the injury to Marcus Rose. He was badly concussed and took no further part in the tour. I was saddened to lose one good friend, but delighted to welcome another in the slightly crumpled shape of the engaging Huw Davies.

Davies was one of the few remaining Corinthians talented enough to prosper in the increasingly serious and committed world of international rugby. He was already in Australia, on tour with Middlesex, and was not exactly thrilled to be called from that tour in the midst of an enjoyable break at Cairns. He was even less enchanted to discover that he had also missed out on England's junket at Hamilton Island. It was the most bizarre scheduling, but again typical of England's haphazard planning, that we should go off for a spot of rest and recreation the day after our opening match. At a time when we should have been focusing all our attention and effort on the forthcoming pool matches, players were paragliding, jet-skiing and generally having a whale of a time. Davies was understandably upset at missing out on both beanfeasts, and was further outraged by a stern wigging from

Martin Green almost as soon as he arrived. His mischievous sense of humour was not appreciated by the coach, who was beginning to fold under the pressure. As a competent club player who was never good enough to have played at international level, Green was full of theory, but short on practical experience.

Despite the defeat by Australia, England duly qualified for the quarter-finals with effortless victories over Japan and the United States. I had played in the latter game and had come on as a replacement for the last five minutes against Japan. Our quarter-final was to be against Wales in Brisbane, and in the light of what had happened on the last occasion the countries had met, it could hardly have been a worse pairing. It was the first time we had played outside Sydney in the competition, which was however something of a relief. We had become strangely isolated in a city where the event was being greeted with studied indifference. It was difficult sometimes to imagine that we were part of the same competition which was enthusing big audiences in New Zealand. It wasn't until that unforgettable semi-final between the Wallabies and France, surely one of the greatest games ever played, that the Australians took the tournament to their hearts. By then it was too late.

I had an inkling beforehand that something was amiss in the Australian camp. The relationship between Alan Jones and some of his senior players was becoming strained. There were too many forceful characters pulling in different directions, too many inflated egos to be satisfied, and it was clear that Jones's sole chance of survival as coach would depend upon Australia's enthronement as world champions. Their defeat by France sealed his fate. His four-year term as national coach was over later that season after a series of disappointing performances against the All Blacks and the Pumas. It was a rancorous end to what had been the most successful period in Australian rugby history. The international game had lost one of its most flamboyant characters and, in his pomp, a truly outstanding coach.

It was a favourite Jones maxim that to win without risk was to triumph without glory. But for the home countries in the 1987 World Cup, any victory, no matter how it was achieved, would be a bonus. England, having lost to Australia, went down ingloriously to Wales. The Irish were beaten by the Wallabies, and Scotland, despite having the better of an exciting draw against France in their pool, were well beaten by the All Blacks. Only Wales, who finished a highly creditable third, could derive any modest satisfaction from the event although they were no match for the eventual champions, New Zealand.

The gap in playing standards between the countries in the two hemispheres was ominously wide and, apparently, getting wider. Our abject performance against a depleted Welsh side signalled the lowest point in my association with England. The Welsh plans had been so seriously disrupted by injury that they had been forced to call in two raw recruits playing club rugby in Canberra, David Young, a prop, and a teenage flanker, Richard Webster. Young was put straight into the team against England. Not only that, but Bob Norster, a key player in the line-out, who had not been entirely blameless in the midst of the mayhem in Cardiff, was not fully fit. On the day before the match, Martin Green had put the English squad through a lengthy, debilitating session, finishing with yet another reminder that there must be no repeat of the violence which had so besmirched the game and the good name of England in Cardiff. One wondered whether the Welsh players had been similarly warned.

Even by our own inconsistent standards in those days, it was a pathetic England performance which once again highlighted the lack of planning and foresight. The turning point was the injury to Paul Rendall just as England were going into a defensive scrummage on their own five-metre line. The reactions from our bench were crucially slow, and before Gareth Chilcott, the replacement, could get on to the field, the scrummage had formed and Gareth Roberts had exploited the numerical weakness in England's back-row defence to score. If England's problems could be encapsulated in a single moment, that would be it.

When the final whistle blew at Ballymore, signalling the end of England's interest in the competition, one or two of the squad sitting in the stand jumped to their feet and cheered. They couldn't wait to get home. England, once proud and mighty, had been reduced to also-rans. In the first ever global tournament England, who had given the game to the world, and who were one of the most powerful nations in terms of playing numbers, weren't in the top four. They probably weren't even in the top six. It had been a sorry humiliation, but saddest of all was the fact that so few people, either within the squad or following the game at home, recognised it as such.

CHAPTER 3

Shaping Up

Once, and so far only once, during my international career have I seriously considered throwing in the towel, and that was in the summer of 1987, after the World Cup. There seemed little point in carrying on chasing a succession of fading rainbows and watching one false dawn after another. The high hopes, the promise of the previous season, had dissolved in the shocking realisation that England were a second-class power in the new world order. The national team were going nowhere and I was going backwards. Despite everything, I had at least completed 1986 as England's first-choice fly half. Now, I was understudy to Peter Williams and, if Stuart Barnes decided to renew his challenge, I could be a distant third.

Everyone had a view on the way ahead but no one seemed to have a clue how to get there. It was a complete void into which I was loath to disappear. And then, two things happened. Peter Williams turned professional, and Mike Weston resigned. Weston had been instrumental in bringing England part of the way into the real world. He had recognised the increasing amount of time and effort the players were devoting to the game and the sacrifices that they were making. He was infinitely more considerate to the players' needs than any of his predecessors. He had also realised the importance of fitness and, in conjunction with Don Rutherford, the Rugby Football Union's technical director, had embarked on devising programmes which would help improve the players' physical condition and their athleticism. The role he had assumed during the World Cup was that of team manager although his title remained Chairman of Selectors. When he returned from Australia, however, he was offered, and accepted, the honorary post of manager. It was a popular choice with the players, who felt that for the first time here was an administrator with their best interests at heart. But within a month or so of his appointment, Weston resigned.

The RFU had refused to accede to his request that Martin Green be retained as a selector. There was no question of Green remaining as a coach. He simply wasn't up to the job, and Weston must have realised that. But when he discovered that he couldn't have Green even as a selector, he did what he considered to be the only honourable thing. Sword-falling is all very well when there is someone coming along behind to clean up the mess, but in England's case the list of possible candidates was decidedly short. There was, in fact, only one name on it – Geoff Cooke. I knew Cooke and admired what he was doing for Yorkshire and particularly for the North, where he had applied his skills to the refinement of the selection process and to the establishment of a management structure comprising just two: himself as manager, and Dave Robinson, a piratical flanker with Gosforth in his day, as coach. Together, they had engineered the North's success in the Divisional Championship, not only in terms of results but in the style in which those results had been achieved. For me the most enjoyable rugby at that time was at county and divisional levels, and Cooke was involved with both. Dare I risk it into the breach one more time?

If Cooke was the outstanding candidate for the managership of England, indeed the only one, his own ideas about how to proceed must have been vaguely defined at that stage. He was a man of strong views who knew what he wanted, but he was, like all of us in the national set-up, feeling his way in a maze. The Divisional Championship was now beginning to assist in the identification of the country's top players and was giving the selectors an opportunity to make a more accurate assessment of players' abilities, but the leagues, which were in their infancy, had not yet had any impact. Cooke possessed a well-organised and analytical mind which was invaluable in those early days of sifting, grading, chopping down and building up. From the start he told us what he wanted for England was success, and that unless the players also shared in that desire, they were wasting their time and his. He quickly introduced the idea of joint responsibility, a startlingly new concept for the old stagers who had blindly accepted the divisive principle of them and us. Here, at last, was the opportunity to give voice to our thoughts and to express our views without fear of retribution. In the bad old days the sharp and, very often, not so short shock for players who had lost form was to drop them, but here was someone advocating player participation. Ye gods, no wonder some of the greyer heads at Twickenham were shaking in disbelief and fury. Not even in the hour of his greatest triumph did Cooke manage to win his detractors round to his way of thinking.

Cooke was taking a massive gamble by insisting that he would do it his way or not at all, that the buck would stop with him and that he would stand or fall by England's results. To most of us who had been on the roller-coaster ride of the last few seasons, he was like a man sitting on a branch with a revolver in one hand and a chainsaw in the other. Underneath were the vultures waiting to devour him should he fall. And he very nearly came a cropper within weeks of his appointment. Having at one stage in his career been employed by a city council, Cooke knew that the surest way of never reaching a decision was to form a committee, and so he ruthlessly set about pruning the numbers involved in national selection from seven to three. His two aides were Roger Uttley, whom he appointed coach, and John Elliott, a former England triallist hooker who had been a divisional selector and who was an astute judge of a player's ability.

Uttley was a good choice as coach. England's greatest need at the time was for a man with the necessary credentials as a player who could command respect and who would return to basics. Incredible as it may seem now, the fundamental principles of ball retention, body positions, angles of running, kickoffs and defensive organisation had never been properly addressed. It is no great secret that Uttley was never in the top bracket as a strategist and that there would come a time when he could take the side no further, but at that stage in the development of the national squad, he was undoubtedly the man for the job.

As part of his team, Cooke also appointed Alan Davies, who had been coach at Nottingham when I was there, and Dave Robinson, as coaches of the B side. They were also in charge of The Rest XV which beat England 13-7 in the trial. I have never been a supporter of trial matches, believing that they pose more questions than they answer, and this match proved my point. Although I had played in the winning side that day, Cooke felt that my rehabilitation from the previous season's traumas was not yet complete and selected Les Cusworth, who was in the midst of an indian summer, for the opening match against France in Paris. There was, unsurprisingly, a strong northern influence in the side which prompted Mark Bailey to remark that the only two requirements for England selection were a flat cap on the head and pigeon shit on the shoulders. Those of us who knew him were pleasantly surprised by the range of Bailey's vocabulary.

In fact, England played well in defeat and had chances enough to have beaten the French comfortably. One of the best was muffed by Will Carling playing in his first international. He missed a glaring overlap and the opportunity of a certain score was lost. Despite this, Carling had good reason to feel satisfied with his game, but at the after-match dinner he was accosted by Peter Winterbottom who told him, in no uncertain terms, exactly what he thought about Carling's decision to run when he should have passed and took the opportunity to introduce the young cub to a few of the facts of life at international level. Winterbottom, strong and silent to the point of being monosyllabic, was probably releasing the pent-up emotion of six years of frustration with England. Perhaps he recognised that this was the start of an exciting new era.

If he did he was in a minority and, following defeat by Wales at Twickenham in the next match, there were even fewer standing up to be counted in Cooke's fast-dwindling band of supporters. He had to win the Calcutta Cup. Mike Harrison, Les Cusworth and the hapless Kevin Simms were dropped. Chris Oti replaced Harrison on the wing, Simon Halliday came into the centre and I was restored at fly half. The captaincy was given to the gifted but injury-prone Nigel Melville. Had Cooke been able to choose a place to make his last stand, it would surely not have been Murrayfield. In recent years there had been simmering resentment when the two sides played, and words were spoken before that match with an intensity of feeling the like of which I have seldom experienced. First Don Rutherford let rip, followed by Melville, normally the most placid of souls, who described the Scots as 'bloody scavengers'. Tom McNab, as proud a Scotsman as ever lived, albeit one who had been assisting the English in their preparations, was standing at the back of the room and was visibly shaken by Melville's venomous outburst. The irony of Melville's remarks was that after an appalling game, which England won 9-6, Derrick Grant, the Scottish coach, blamed England for ruining the contest as a spectacle, accusing us of killing the ball. With Winterbottom on one side of the scrum and Gary Rees on the other, Grant may have had a point, but it was a classic case of the pot calling the kettle black.

For England and for Cooke it was a win and that, for the moment, would suffice, although neither Cooke nor Uttley was greatly enchanted by the quality of our play. 'Could do a lot better,' was Cooke's summary. In the next game against Ireland we were to show him exactly what we could do.

This was the day when Cooke convinced all but his most implacable critics that he was guiding England along the right track. We produced forty minutes of fluent rugby. Six tries, three of them by Chris Oti in his second international, two for Rory, and from the midst of a crowd intoxicated by the splendour of it all came, for the first time at Twickenham, in almost mystic unison, the strains of 'Swing low . . . '. Cooke's chariot was beginning to roll. But it had been at a price. Nigel Melville had dislocated his ankle and was carried from the field in agony just before half time. It was a sickening sight, his foot twisted at a grotesque angle, and quite the worst injury in what was a catalogue of hideous misfortune for England's captain. We were 3-0 down at the time and despite the fact that Richard Harding's arrival coincided with a dramatic upturn in our fortunes, I don't believe that it was his presence alone which turned the possible into the perfect. To this day it remains one of the most liberating forty minutes of rugby I have ever played. All I know is that there was a kind of emotional bonding between the team during half time. We had a responsibility to ourselves, and now a duty to Melville, to go out and win this game and to win it in a manner which would have gained his approval.

A thousand years is reason enough for a party, and the Irish, who seldom need any excuse, celebrated Dublin's birthday with the Millennium Match against England at Lansdowne Road. We beat them again, not so convincingly this time, but comfortably enough. Three wins in a row was a new experience for me as it was, I imagine, for everyone else in the side. But we were still in the foothills. The summit was a long way up and after the tour to Australia in that summer of 1988, the mountain seemed unscalable. Australia were no great shakes themselves. Alan Jones had been replaced as coach by Bob Dwyer, and he had barely started the task of rebuilding for the next World Cup, in 1991.

In selecting his touring party, Geoff Cooke made some major misjudgements. Chief of these was the appointment of John Orwin as captain. Orwin had led the side in Nigel Melville's absence during the second half against Ireland at Twickenham and again in the Millennium Match. He was a good, grafting forward and a reliable jumper at the front of the line-out. He may have had some limited experience of command during his years in the RAF, but he lacked the personality and the sensitivity to captain an international rugby side. He was temperamentally unsuited to the job, suffering from severe bouts of self-importance. On one occasion he burst through a queue of players waiting for physiotherapy and, ordering John Bentley off the treatment table, demanded that Kevin Murphy, our physiotherapist, give him priority as captain. Murphy refused. As the tour progressed Orwin became more and more detached from his players and when Will Carling, who had been delayed at home by exams, belatedly joined the party, his greeting from the captain was less than friendly – 'Good of you to turn up,' he said. They were the only words he spoke to Carling on the tour. Orwin was every bit as disastrous a choice as captain in Australia as John Scott had been in South Africa four years earlier. Cooke committed other errors. He was still finding his feet as a selector and inevitably he would make miscalculations on his way to determining the best combination. Once again he fell into the trap of picking too many northerners, a number of whom were not, and never would be, international class. Ray Adamson, the Wakefield full back, was one, and others who were to fall quickly by the wayside included Simon Robson, the Moseley scrum half, Barry Evans, the Leicester wing, and the Yorkshire centre John Bentley, who later turned professional.

It was Bentley's interception of a Michael Lynagh pass which propelled England to a 13-3 lead against the Wallabies in the First Test at Brisbane. Earlier in the game Nick Farr-Jones, of all people, had presented Bryan Barley with the gift of an interception from which Rory scored. But Australia kept their cool and won 22-16. They had much less trouble in winning the Second Test in Sydney 28-8. Before that game the players had called a meeting for a heart-to-heart chat. Orwin, to his credit, had been one of the instigators. We talked about pride in performance and about our refusal to accept second best. We were forced to accept second best in that series, nevertheless I was encouraged by the attitude shown by the players. I also believed that out of the defeat in Australia would come victory. It was the last I would see of some of those players in an England jersey, but I could never have imagined that it would be the last I would see of my old rival, Barnes, for five years.

I don't know what it was he did or when he did it, but I can only surmise that Will Carling had done something on that tour of Australia to convince Cooke that he was the man to lead England into the nineties and through the World Cup in 1991. It was a long leasehold on a job which previously had no security of tenure. If ever I was going to be offered the captaincy, I suppose it was then, going into the 1988–89 season. There had been speculation in the press that it would be me and the thought had, of course, crossed my mind. But I can honestly say that when Carling's appointment was announced I was pleased for him. There was, I suppose, a twinge of personal disappointment but no more than that. To be frank, I was not at all certain that I deserved the position. I had not played with any degree of consistency. For every couple of things I did well I made a mistake. There was also the constant sight of Barnes in my rear-view mirror. I couldn't be sure of my place. That was not a problem which confronted Carling and so, at the age of twenty-two, he became England's youngest captain for fifty-seven years. His first assignment was to lead us against Nick Farr-Jones's Wallabies who had arrived that autumn. The fact that all but one of the English divisions, the Midlands, had beaten the tourists was not necessarily a good omen for England. But there had been some stirring performances which Cooke could not ignore. For the North there was an unheralded scrum half from Winnington Park, Dewi Morris, a Welshman who was to give his heart and soul to England every time he played for them. He scored a fine try in the North's 15-9 win. Even more impressive was Paul Ackford who, at the relatively advanced age of thirty, after ten years of unfulfilled promise, was belatedly reaching his full potential as a second-row forward. He had played magnificently for Harlequins in the cup final the previous season against Bristol and was now continuing that form for London.

The Wallabies, who must have realised that the tour was on the brink of collapse, sent for Michael Lynagh, who had been injured and was unavailable for selection in the original party. But not even Lynagh's touch could save Australia that day against England. With Carling the darling of the Twickenham crowd, England won in spectacular style 28-19. It was now obvious to me that Cooke had a sharper understanding of the players he wanted for England and of the game he wanted them to play. There was a collective appreciation of what we were trying to achieve. There were, in addition, all the qualities which had been missing for so long – loyalty, pride and respect. Above all there was continuity and consistency in selection.

The combinations were coming together. In the front row there was the luxury of three top-class props in Rendall, Chilcott and Probyn, with Moore between them at hooker. Ackford and Dooley were very obviously going to be a formidable pair at lock. And although the back-row balance wasn't ideal against Australia, there were flankers of the calibre of Teague, Skinner and, of course, Winterbottom, who had been in South Africa, lining up to join number eight Dean Richards. I was satisfied that I had found a natural partner in Dewi Morris who had made such a strong impression during his international début against the Australians. There were still some rough edges to his game but the natural talent was there and there could be no question about his commitment.

A bit like Morris, however, England weren't yet the finished article. Not by a long chalk. We also had to cope with a new phenomenon, media hype. It was during our training break in Lanzarote, prior to the 1989 Five Nations Championship, that the press began to write us up. Carling had made several positive statements about England's chances which, by the time they appeared in print, were arrogant contortions of what he had really said. That, at least, was how they were interpreted by the Scots against whom we were defending the Calcutta Cup, or the Calcutta Plate, as it had become known after its part in an unsheduled kick-about the previous season between John Jeffrey, Dean Richards and half the revellers in Edinburgh's Rose Street.

The enmity between the two countries had escalated alarmingly both on and off the field. Not only did it manifest itself in the matches but it was also seriously disrupting the administrative unity of the four Home Unions. Childish behaviour from the players may, at times, be excusable; less so from those running the game.

This was the day when the Scots gained full revenge for our alleged spoiling tactics at Murrayfield the previous season. They came with no thought other than to prevent us from playing the brand of rugby which had demoralised the Wallabies. They had the players to do it. John Jeffrey's entire career was played on the edge of legality, and he spent most of this match on the wrong side of the law. He and Finlay Calder, another pocket-picker, took Andy Robinson out of the game. Robinson had been highly effective against Australia but was drawn into a private battle he couldn't hope to win. Frustration for him, frustration for Jon Webb and me, we missed seven kicks between us, and frustration for England, who failed to raise their game to levels which would have been too rarefied for the Scots. The result was a wholly unsatisfactory 12-12 draw. No Triple Crown, no Grand Slam this year. Instead another lesson, another stepping stone.

There were also some lessons for our new captain. I knew only too well how quickly the media could turn from sycophants to savages but it was a new experience for Carling. The first lesson he received was how futile it is to criticise the press. One story from the archives has always remained with me. It was from the 1977 Lions tour of New Zealand which, by all accounts, was one of the most miserably unhappy trips in the Lions' history. John Dawes, the successful captain of the 1971 Lions and already an icon in the world game, was the much less successful coach in 1977. He and Clem Thomas, then the *Observer*'s rugby correspondent, were having an argument over something Thomas had written. 'I'll ruin you, Thomas,' said Dawes. 'Wrong,' replied Thomas. 'I'll be around long after the game has finished with you.'

Now it was Carling's turn to discover that the power of the press operates in two ways, for you or against you. There had been criticism of England's tactical inflexibility against the Scots, yet few had expected Carling at this stage in his captaincy to conjure up a brilliant ploy which would have altered the pattern of play and changed the course of the match. Our forwards, however, were less forgiving and before the Irish game, after some horseplay amongst the backs, Dean Richards took Carling aside for a quiet word. There was no question of Carling not taking the game or his position as captain seriously. It is simply that we all have different ways of releasing tension. The forwards are a breed apart and that is reflected in their match preparations. The backs tend to have other ways of psyching themselves up for the big occasion. The point is that forwards and backs are not two separate entities who happen to run on at the same time to the same field only to perform different functions when they get there. The modern game has moved on from that, with the one group willing and able to do the other's job. Nothing infuriates me more than this absurd distinction between forwards and backs, the one mean, macho and match-winners, the other limp-wristed dandies. It is old-fashioned tribal nonsense which does nothing for the game. There are few more physically demanding positions than the midfield, where speed and mass meet in explosive collision.

It was obvious from the Scottish game that we were not yet ready to meet the high expectations of our press and public. We had been manifestly superior to the Scots but had been sucked into an attritional battle from which there was no escape. England and Carling regained some of the lost ground in the next match, against Ireland in Dublin. There was an incident, however, the echoes of which return to haunt us to this day. Midway through the second half, with Ireland still in the game, we were awarded a penalty. I wanted to take the kick at goal but instead Carling ordered a tap penalty from which Brian Moore scored. On this occasion the end had justified the means, but it was to be a different story a year later at Murrayfield.

We didn't deserve the outcome of the final game of that season, which hit us like an avalanche. Or did we? True, we hadn't played well against Scotland but we had gone on to beat Ireland and France with reasonable ease. We therefore went to Cardiff with every hope of winning the championship. The Welsh were still living on time borrowed from their glorious past. It was twenty-six years since England had won in Cardiff and now, surely, was the time to end the nation's suffering. We should not however have gone into the game without Jeff Probyn. He had been concussed against Ireland, yet despite missing the French game, his enforced period of rest was over in time to play Wales, and he was back in the Wasps side, fully recovered. Cooke and Uttley had been reluctant to change a winning team, which was understandable but which took no account of Mike Griffiths's scrummaging strength. Against Gareth Chilcott, who was a specialist loose head converted to the tight, that was crucial. So was the head injury early in the game to Mike Teague. His departure allowed Bob Norster to rule the line-out. Robert Jones ran the show from scrum half and England were again the blushing bridesmaids. Blushing certainly because the decisive score, albeit a controversial one, by Mike Hall, came as the result of a cock-up between Rory and Jon Webb. There was panic under a high ball and in the confusion Rory's pass to Webb went astray. But England could hardly complain. On the bleakest of Cardiff days, Wales won the major share of possession, held the territorial advantage and deserved to win the match.

So many times the light at the end of our tunnel had been attached to an oncoming train that Cooke must have wondered if we were ever going to emerge from the gloom. We were getting closer, but the mental barrier of translating our superiority into victory was still the problem. There was always next season. Not quite, because there was still some unfinished business at the rump of this one.

The Lions were going to Australia but, infuriatingly, not with me in the party. I had been omitted from the original selection, which was both a surprise and a disappointment. It was obvious during the course of the championship that the main body of the party would be made up of English and Scottish players and I felt that I had played as well, if not better, than the other contenders, Paul Dean of Ireland and the Scotsman, Craig Chalmers, who was in his first season of international rugby. In the event, I believe that I was the sacrifice in the political carve-up which usually attends Lions selection, and Dean and Chalmers were the chosen two. There was compensation of sorts with the announcement of the England team to play Romania, although whether playing in Bucharest in spring can ever be thought of as a consoling prospect is questionable. For one thing the heat at that time of year is almost intolerable.

Still under the yoke of Nicolae Ceauşescu, the country was impoverished and poorly equipped to host an international team of players accustomed to luxury and a bit of pampering. Everywhere there were signs of Ceauşescu's evil regime. Dingy apartment blocks, ill-lit roads and, around every corner, men in black leather coats. There was an atmosphere of suspicion and menace. The Romanians, with their glorious architecture and cultural heritage, are a proud nation who had been reduced to wretchedness by one man's inhumanity to his fellows. The most moving example of the depths to which they had sunk was the moment when one of the waiters in our hotel asked if we would give him a Mars bar, not for himself, but for a birthday treat for his son. It is the inevitable consequence of privilege that we take our good fortune and our position as international sportsmen so much for granted.

I was to captain England for the first time. Will Carling, who had been suffering for most of the season with painful shins, had been told that he had a stress fracture and the only cure was a long rest. He would miss not only the Romanian match but also the Lions tour. His absence meant that Jeremy Guscott would win his first cap. Guscott's skills had already been recognised. He had been picked for the Lions and his elevation to full English status was only a matter of time. The other new caps were Simon Hodgkinson at full back and my club partner, Steve Bates, at scrum half. It was to be an auspicious occasion for all three. Romania were not to be taken lightly. They had beaten Wales in Cardiff earlier in the season but, in the enervating heat of Bucharest that day, our forwards were irresistible. Guscott produced the most sensational display of rugby pyrotechnics, scoring three tries, Chris Oti scored four and Hodgkinson succeeded with nine kicks from ten attempts. The result, 58-3, was one of the most satisfying of my career.

CHAPTER 4

Armageddon

I imagined that the changing room at Murrayfield had altered very little since England first played on the ground sixty-five years earlier. It was a barn of a place, almost big enough to accommodate a game of five-a-side football. I wondered how many England fly halves before me had pulled their jerseys from the very peg that I was using now. One thing I knew for sure. None of them had ever been in my position of going out against the Old Enemy with both sides in pursuit of Europe's ultimate prize, the Grand Slam. Despite the Scots' home advantage, England were the firm favourites. Tickets for what was, with some justification, billed as the Match of the Century were selling on the black market at preposterously inflated prices. It was a unique occasion and one for which I felt that England were fully prepared.

Apart from a sluggish first half against Ireland in the opening championship match of the 1990 season, we had played with confidence, style and character. The latter quality had been put to the severest test, as it so often was, against France in Paris. Our training session on the Friday, conducted by the players themselves, had been the slickest I could remember. Every pass went to hand, every kick was spot-on, every catch was held and every run was angled to perfection on a balmy Parisian morning. The next day we awoke to menacing grey skies and gale-force winds. In the stadium adjacent to Parc des Princes where our B side had been playing France B earlier in the day, the roof had been torn off the indoor tennis court. Simon Hodgkinson and I walked out on to the pitch before the match and our hearts sank. Hodgkinson, as the first-choice goal kicker, had the greater responsibility but the accuracy and control of my tactical kicking was essential to our game plan. It was also vitally important to my peace of mind, and against opponents who might offer no more than a handful of scoring opportunities during the match, we felt that the game could be won or lost by the quality of our kicking, whether it was out of the hand or off the ground.

I don't think I have ever witnessed a more extraordinary display of goal kicking than the one Hodgkinson produced that afternoon. His technique and his temperament stood foursquare against the elements. It is when the wind blows on the golf course that the men are separated from the boys, and only the best survive. In Paris, Hodgkinson was a world beater. He kicked two early penalties which had the dual effect of settling us and unnerving the volatile French.

Over the years they had worked hard at improving their discipline but it was still possible to rattle them. We had targeted the two players we considered most important to France, Serge Blanco and Pierre Berbizier. Berbizier was the one who pulled the strings. Tactically aware, he possessed a keen understanding of the game and its laws. It had been from his astuteness that France had scored a try from a quick throw-in in the very first minute of their game against Scotland in 1986. Get to Berbizier and you were halfway to getting to France. At scrum half he had a tighter cordon of security around him than Blanco, who was never at his best under the high ball. I began the deliberate softening-up process with a series of kicks aimed at Blanco. The majority of them were accurate enough for our loose forwards to make their hits, and Blanco began to display signs of extreme distaste for this kind of treatment. Then Carling put in a withering tackle on Berbizier, a fraction late, I grant you, but the combined effects of this physical pounding were starting to tell.

Gradually I felt that I had the extra second of time, the extra metre of space that can make such a difference. The forwards were producing quality ball and behind them Richard Hill was doing what he did best. His pass was fast, straight and true. He was twice the player throughout the second phase of his international career, and it was from his whipped pass under pressure that I found room on the blind side. I kicked down the touch line and Rory, blazing along the wing, scored our first try. Jeremy Guscott slid over for a second and Carling, with almost contemptuous ease, rounded a by now very irritable Blanco for the third. The French were, by this time, a rabble, a spent force, no longer the intimidating invincibles who had come strutting out on to the field before kickoff.

Paris is the only place where the two teams enter the gladiatorial arena side by side, and it was always a mystery to me why the French came on looking as if they had already played. They were sweating profusely, their shirts soaked in a mixture of grease and perspiration. Excitable Frogs, I thought, in my naivety. It was only later in my career that I realised there is a full-sized gymnasium attached to the French dressing room, and the team spend the half-hour before kick off working themselves up into a lather.

There was nothing like a gymnasium attached to the old dressing room at Murrayfield. A piece of faded matting frayed by millions of studs was our warming-up pad before that game of games in 1990. Strange, but I didn't feel as nervous as I thought I would. Perhaps that was the trouble. Certainly Mark Bailey and one or two others who were on the England bench spoke afterwards of a complacency which had begun to settle over the team on the Friday afternoon and was still apparent on the morning of the match. At the time they had interpreted it as genuine confidence. We had every reason to feel confident. Our demolition of Wales a month before had been as complete as any English victory in recent memory. It had led to the resignation of the Welsh coach John Ryan, whose successor Ron Waldron from Neath, then the most successful club side in Wales, had packed the national side with Neath players for the game against Scotland. Having that weekend off, the England squad watched the match on television. Mistake number one. The Scots struggled to beat the side we had destroyed. Subconsciously we may have begun to feel that the Grand Slam was already ours. It wasn't that we underrated the Scots. Far from it. They had, in David Sole, John Jeffrey, Finlay Calder and their half backs Gary Armstrong and Craig Chalmers, the driving forces in the team. They had a world-class full back in Gavin Hastings and, in Ian McGeechan, one of the shrewdest coaches in the world. We knew that they would have done their homework. But we still believed that with the awesome power of our forwards we would be able to play the game on our terms. There was just no way their jumpers could cope with the likes of Ackford and Dooley in head-on confrontation at the line-out. We also had the superior scrummage, which meant that we could adopt the patterns which had systematically destroyed Ireland, France and Wales. Like our training in Paris a month previously, the session at Peebles the day before the match went like clockwork. Bill McLaren, who was watching, shook his head. 'Aye, lads,' he said, doling out the inevitable Hawick Balls. 'We'll hae a job tae beat you tomorrow.' It was, I think, a genuine expression of admiration.

Mistake number two was Peebles. We had made the same error in Wales when we used to stay at Chepstow and travelled into Cardiff for the first time on match day. Going cold into Edinburgh which, on that Saturday in March, was crackling with electricity, came as a shock to the system. Richard Hill and I walked on to the pitch when we arrived at the ground just to sample the atmosphere, which even then was different from anything we had experienced before. The noise levels from the stands and the terraces would be deafening. We'd have to shout our instructions to each other even from a couple of yards' range. But I had no doubts about the efficiency of our communication system at half back.

Hill and I always shared a room for international matches and we had spent hours planning for this day. We had drawn up diagrams plotting our moves from different positions on the field. We had at least three options for each position depending upon the conditions, the match situation, quality of possession, etc. But that season we had regularly run into problems with the forwards. We had a definite communication problem between 8, 9 and 10. Dean Richards had not played in the Five Nations Championship because of injury and Mike Teague, who had performed so superbly on the blind side for the Lions the previous summer, was switched to number eight. At team meetings when we discussed the various manoeuvres for half backs and three-quarters, there were mutterings amongst the forwards, who felt that the final decision should be left to them. The backs had a powerful ally in captain Carling, nevertheless I had a vague feeling of unease that, in a crisis, we might be overruled.

Never, surely, in the history of the game has a match, a season and a nation's fate hinged to such an extent on one moment's aberration as in this tempestuous contest. The Scots, as we knew they would, had planned meticulously. They lost no opportunity to break up our rhythm and disrupt our line-out. Their jumpers interchanged with baffling facility from back to front to middle, and on one occasion, Calder surreptitiously appeared at the front to make off with the ball before anyone knew what was happening. Our discipline, normally so controlled, deserted us temporarily, and Scotland kicked two penalties.

If international rugby has taught me anything in the last ten years, it is that a lead, no matter how fragile, is a precious commodity. Six points down, with a strong wind blowing in the Scots' favour, may not seem much, but it was six points we were going to have to score to get back into the game, and against ferociously committed opponents, who would rather die than miss a tackle, that was never going to be easy. Therefore, when the opportunity came for England to make up for lost ground, we should have taken it. That is said in the comfort and security of hindsight. At the time I felt that Carling's decision to preserve our territorial advantage and keep the pressure on the Scottish scrummage, rather than attempt the kicks at goal, was the correct one. For one thing the wind facing us was strong enough to make kicking a lottery. Simon Hodgkinson had already refused the invitation to take one kick and, had he missed with any one of the subsequent penalties awarded to England, it would have enabled the Scots to clear their lines, relieve the pressure, and set up an attacking position for themselves in our half. The second point is that the strength of our scrummaging was beginning to take its toll on the Scots. Derek White, a key figure in the Scots' plans, had been injured and his replacement by Derek Turnbull forced the Scots to reorganise their back row.

Much has been made of Carling's apparent indecision and his surrender to Brian Moore on the question of whether to scrum or to kick for goal. But this was an occasion, an atmosphere, that none of us had ever previously experienced. The noise, the pace, the physical commitment, added to the emotional intensity, were too much for one man, and one man, remember, who was himself a relative newcomer, not only to captaincy but to international rugby. He wanted advice, he needed support, and at the time most of us felt he had made the right choice. The fact that I, for one, now feel differently is irrelevant to the decisions which were taken in the white-hot heat of the moment at Murrayfield that day. In any case, when Guscott scored his try after a classic drive by the England forwards, it scarcely seemed to matter. This had been our game plan. To use our loose forwards to commit the Scottish forwards and to keep them tied down out of the way of our backs. It had worked beautifully for Guscott's try, and there was no reason to believe that it wouldn't work again through a second half when the wind advantage would be ours. Not even a third Scottish penalty just before half time could dampen our spirits, which rose appreciably when the Scots kicked out on the full at the restart, and we were given a scrummage on the halfway line.

Hill and I knew exactly what to do in this situation. No need even to check with each other. I had been delighted with my kicking into the wind and here was a chance, much earlier than expected, to work us down to near the Scottish line. Before he put the ball into the scrum, Hill glanced up to see where I was standing. A fast delivery right of centre. He knew precisely what I wanted. In my mind's eye I could see my kick spiralling down into the Scottish twenty-two where we would pitch camp for the rest of the game. There was no counter-command from the forwards. The ball went into the front row, through the second row, and was at Teague's feet. What went through his mind remains a mystery. The forwards claim that they called a back-row move but to have done so from that position and in that situation broke every rule of conventional strategy. Teague knocked on, the Scots won the scrum and, irony of ironies, employing the same kind of back-row move which England had so disastrously attempted seconds before, broke through to score the try which settled the match. It takes seconds to write, took seconds to score but the effect has left a permanent scar on the minds of those of us playing for England that day.

Geoff Cooke has often said that the words 'if only' are the two most useless in the English language. He is right. But how often since that afternoon at Murrayfield have we used them. If only we had kicked our penalties when they were offered, then perhaps there would have been less pressure on Teague. If only the forwards had told us what they had planned. If only, if only, if only . . . All I know is that no one, apart from the fifteen Englishmen on the field, can even begin to imagine the numbing helplessness we felt when the final whistle blew. The Scottish crowd swept past us in their crazed rush to capture a glimpse of their heroes, as the untouchables from England were left to find their way off the field as quickly and as anonymously as they could.

I hope that I never again have to experience the utter despair of the England changing room after that game. No one moved, no one spoke. Words were superfluous, bodies were too tired, too sore to move. The first sound after what seemed like an eternity was the tab being peeled from a beer can. There were other signs of life. The click of a cigarette lighter, the hiss of more beer cans, and then Carling spoke. 'Listen, lads. We have taken part in a great occasion. We have done bloody magnificently to get here and no one can take that from us. Remember too that no one outside this room can possibly know or understand what we've been through this season. What we feel here, now, is for us and us alone, and because of it we'll be all the stronger in the future.' Mature words from a young man in only his second season of captaincy. For Carling, and for England, things were to get worse before they got better.

CHAPTER 5

Into Orbit

'Call for you, Rob – it's Will Carling.' Business was booming, I was working round the clock, and had it been anyone else on the other end of the office telephone, I would have made some excuse. But I had a hunch that this might be a very important call. The Divisional Championship in that 1990–91 season marked the lowest point in Carling's reign as captain. After the Murrayfield defeat, the press had gone to war on him, tearing him down from the pedestal on to which they had lifted him just two short seasons before. He had been singled out for criticism, quite unfairly in my opinion, and blamed for England's tactical ineptness against Scotland. The criticism was relentless and now, after the glory, Carling was beginning to experience the less acceptable face of public life. He didn't know how to handle it. Nor was there to be any release during the summer, when England set off on one of the most ill-starred ventures of recent times to Argentina.

The Falklands War was still a bitter memory for many Argentinians, and feelings often rose unpleasantly to the surface during the tour. Union Jacks were burned at matches and there were many other demonstrations of lingering bitterness. This, on top of all the other problems associated with touring, was too much for Carling and, at times, for the England management. Matters were not helped by the fact that the touring party wasn't up to full strength. Quite a few of us who had been with the Lions the previous summer in Australia decided not to tour, believing that with the hectic playing schedule in the coming months which would culminate in the World Cup, a break from rugby was essential. I was also influenced in my decision to stay at home that summer by the fact that Sara was expecting our first child in July. After five years of almost continuous competitive

47

rugby, I wanted to be with her and to play some recreational cricket. When I received a call from a beleaguered Geoff Cooke in Buenos Aires asking me if I would join the tour as a replacement, I politely declined.

The Argentine tour was Carling's first as captain. He soon learned that leading a touring side is a very different proposition to captaincy at home. There are so many additional responsibilities, so many other duties to discharge. On tour, where there is no hiding place, the captain is constantly on show and never far from the public gaze. The problems are greatly magnified if the team are not performing well on the field and, despite sharing the test series with the Pumas, it could, by no stretch of the imagination, be described as a successful tour. Of the new breed of developing players, only Jason Leonard was to come through. It was a grave disappointment to the management, who found themselves under severe pressure.

That tour also marked the beginning of the deterioration in the relationship between Carling and Roger Uttley, and even Geoff Cooke showed signs of strain. Carling felt that England, having reached the level of the previous season, now needed to advance to a higher plane, and he was frustrated by Uttley's seeming inability to do that. But in fairness to Uttley on that tour, he had a hard enough job implanting the fundamental skills into many of his rawer recruits. Unfortunately for Carling, the end of the tour did not bring an end to his own problems.

He had steered England successfully through early-season games against the Barbarians and, in what was sweet revenge for the summer's indignities, the Pumas. The Pumas had gone down all right – 51-0 – but not, alas, without a fight. Their eighteen-year-old prop Federico Mendez was sent off after knocking Paul Ackford senseless with a haymaker. I doubt that Ackford, one of the hard men of the English pack, will ever live down the ignominy of being flattened by a schoolboy's punch. Some punch, some schoolboy.

Both games had provided the test bed for England's new strategy that season. Our experiences the previous season had taught us the harsh reality that pretty rugby doesn't win the top prizes. It had been attractive to watch, fun to play, but it had achieved nothing. This time it would be different. Winning was to be our sole objective and if that meant playing a game of limited ambition through the grinding power of our forwards and the kicking of our half backs, so be it. Nothing would deflect us from our chosen course. The 1991 Five Nations campaign has been described as a joyless one and, to an extent, it was. But unlike every other championship series for more than a decade, it was a triumphant one for England, and to those of us who had come up with the side from the gloomy depths of the mid eighties, that was all that mattered. Our blueprint for success, put into practice against the Barbarians and Argentina, had worked, and that was deeply satisfying, but nothing, it seemed, could lift Carling's spirits. The form which had begun to desert him in Argentina had still not returned, and matters came to a head during the Divisional Championship when he was dropped by Dick Best as a reprimand for failing to attend a London training session. It was a simple misunderstanding, but whilst I had a certain sympathy for Carling I had, as captain of London, a loyalty to my coach and to my players. I recognised immediately, however, that it was the worst possible thing for Carling. The press were itching to have another go at him and now he had given them the opportunity. The incident further damaged his public image. I knew that Carling was a very confused, very depressed young man.

I also knew the reason for his phone call to the office. He wanted to relinquish the captaincy of England. As we talked, the buzz around me in the office became hushed almost to the point of total silence. It was as if everyone was aware of the gravity of the situation. I don't know to what extent I was able to influence Carling in his final decision but I am certain that he was just this one phone call away from offering his resignation to Geoff Cooke.

I told him that whatever he did, he must not act on impulse. He first had to consider where England had come from, where they were now and what they had achieved under his leadership. Each season under his captaincy England had improved their position. I also told him that if he chucked in the towel, he would have conceded victory to the press and surrendered to the campaign of criticism which had brought him to this state of uncertainty and insecurity. I felt that Carling had been the victim of a vendetta which had begun gently with one or two comments but was now rapidly gaining an irresistible momentum. It had happened to me in the past, as it was to do again later in my career, but at least I could talk from experience which, I hoped, might help him. If he could survive this and come through it, in all probability he would emerge a better player and a more mature person. Jon Webb, Simon Hodgkinson and Dewi Morris had all done so after suffering similar disparagement.

As someone who genuinely believed that Carling was the man best suited for the job, I implored him not to give up the captaincy. All the time that I was listening, persuading, cajoling, pleading, I realised that if Carling did resign, the person most likely to be appointed as his successor was me. There had been speculation in the press, talk in the office, and there had been times, I confess, when I had hoped that it would happen. But never had I been more certain in my belief that, for the good of the players, for the good of the team, and for the good of English rugby, Carling had to remain as captain.

The 1991 Championship was almost upon us when we set off for Lanzarote. During our five days of sunshine training, the feeling grew ever stronger that this was to be England's year for the Grand Slam, although I doubted at this stage whether we were good enough as a side or confident enough as individuals to be certain of winning the World Cup, unlike the Australians, who had never entertained the notion of coming second.

It is one thing to speak blithely of winning World Cups. It is another to know how to do it. We had to identify specific areas for improvement: goal kicking, contact work, angles of running and, not least, psychological motivation. Cooke, like Carling, knew that England had to move forward from their position of the previous season. Fitness monitoring and dietary control had become accepted as important elements in the development and improvement of the modern rugby player, and now Cooke introduced such novelties as goal setting, mental rehearsals, concentration training and anxiety control. Many in the squad were sceptical and remained so, but I found that it helped me. I began to get an overall picture of the game I was about to play. I could visualise certain positions on the field where I knew what was going to happen and what I would have to do. Cooke, through his psychological motivation, was encouraging us to look beyond the obvious, but too few, in my opinion, were prepared to see further than the next set piece.

Going to Cardiff two days before the match, rather than on the Saturday morning as had been our custom, was part of Cooke's psychological build-up for the opening Championship game against Wales. Our preparations had begun on the Wednesday evening at Kingsholm in Gloucester where the manager had organised a special

St David's Day welcome for us. As we ran on to the field the tannoy crackled into life with a scratchy rendition of the Welsh national anthem. As we crossed the Severn Bridge the following day, the anthem was played again on the team bus, and for the next forty-eight hours, we were immersed in all things Welsh. By the time we walked through the packed lobby of our hotel an hour and a half before kickoff and began our solemn march to the ground through thousands of milling supporters, we were totally immune to the Welsh and to Wales.

Sombre but determined. That was the mood in the squad before the match, the only light relief brought unwittingly to the proceedings by Richard Hill, who had been asked by Carling to express some thoughts on the forthcoming game at the team meeting on the Friday night. Unfortunately the red mists descend over Hill at the very mention of Wales, rendering normal speech quite impossible. Such was the torrent of outraged abuse which poured from him that we were reduced to uncontrollable fits of laughter and the meeting broke up in disarray. Carling tried again with Hill before the Irish match but the same thing happened. Hill had to work very hard to keep control of his emotions and it was vital for all of us that he did. The signs were not encouraging when he and Robert Jones squared up to each other and indulged in a bout of vigorous finger-wagging before the kickoff.

Even less auspicious was our start. Brian Moore needlessly gave away a penalty at the kickoff, Dean Richards fumbled Neil Jenkins's miscued kick for touch, and seconds later we had conceded another penalty in front of our posts which Paul Thorburn converted. Three points down within a minute, and as the half progressed, things didn't get any better. We were sluggish, we were off the pace and we were still giving away penalties. Carling and Dooley exchanged a few unpleasantries after one of the many indiscretions, and Thorburn was given a chance to put Wales further ahead. Fortunately for us he missed, as he was to do another three times in the first half, but we stuck to our plan, relentlessly narrow as it was, and gradually began to pull clear. The Welsh choirs had lost their voices and very soon there would be no crowd. Long before the final whistle they had begun to drift away, disenchanted as much with the monotony of the spectacle as with Wales's impending defeat. We couldn't have cared less. We had come to do a job. And we had done it with the precision and clinical efficiency of a military operation. In and out with a victory which had eluded England for twenty-eight years. The relief was enormous, the ghosts of past horrors in Cardiff had finally been laid to rest.

It had been decided before the game that England would not attend the traditional after-match press conference. It was, we all later agreed, a wrong decision. But the reasoning behind it had seemed sound enough at the time. There was no malice intended, but win, lose or draw, Cooke and Carling did not want to be ambushed or stampeded into making rash remarks they might afterwards regret. The press hype in the days leading up to the game had been every bit as inflammatory as it was before the Calcutta Cup the previous season. What we did not know at the time was that the affair would be complicated by and confused with demands made by our agent, Bob Willis, to BBC television for money for the players' pool. It was a sensitive issue. Relations between the players and the Rugby Football Union on the subject of financial remuneration were almost at breaking point, and Cooke was severely censured. Some at headquarters never forgave him for his actions that day in Cardiff.

What should have been a historic milestone in English rugby history and a cause for celebration had been soured by bitterness and controversy. For the players, however, it was no more than a minor irritation. We were proud of what we had done in Cardiff, although we knew that it was merely the first step on what would be a long and arduous journey to the World Cup. The job we had performed efficiently and without emotion against Wales would now have to be repeated at Twickenham against the Scots. The game plan we had devised for the season was tailor-made to scupper Scotland. Of all our opponents they had been the most cussedly difficult to beat. They had grown fat on our pickings and, over the years, we had given them plenty to feed off. However much we had attempted to expand our game, the Scots had managed to thwart us. Their back row were past masters at profiting from unconsidered trifles and their midfield defence was as tough to crack as any in the Championship. But this time we gave them nothing. Our forwards drove remorselessly, and if Hill didn't pin them down in the corners, then I did.

I had sensed even before the kick-off that this was to be England's day. Lining up waiting to be presented to the Princess Royal, you could tell from the Scots' eyes that they lacked the fanatical fervour of the previous season. It turned out to be one of my easiest internationals. With Ackford and Dooley swallowing up all our line-out ball – and most of the opposition's as well – I had the ultimate luxury of kicking when and where I pleased.

It was not a luxury afforded to me in the next match, against Ireland at Lansdowne Road. A combination of rain and Ireland's abrasive forwards made our lives a misery for all but the last seven minutes of the game. The sense of *déjà vu* just after half time, when Ireland did almost precisely what the Scots had done the season before, was terrifyingly vivid. Tony Stanger, the Scottish wing, had wrecked us then, and Simon Geoghegan, with that swashbuckling pace of his, looked as if he had finished us off now with a lovely try in the corner. Until Rory, with what he will go to his grave believing was his most important try for England, saved us with a piece of wizardry manufactured out of thin air. At least we hadn't panicked this time. We had fretted a lot, though, and there were some harsh words coming back from the forwards, who felt that my kicking wasn't up to scratch. But at no time had we despaired of victory. Almost as important as Rory's try and Hodgkinson's goal kicking was Nigel Heslop's kick out of defence which had gained sixty yards from the tightest of angles. From there, the forwards had pummelled the Irish midfield, softening them up for Rory's lethal finishing thrust.

At last, after eleven barren years of frustration, criticism and, occasionally, ridicule, England had won something. The Triple Crown had been our minimum objective that season but the effect on our supporters was immediate. For as long as I could remember, since winning my first cap against Romania in 1985, the arrival of the team bus at Twickenham had been greeted with supreme indifference by the occupants of the West car park, who were much too interested in their Chablis and smoked salmon to be distracted by anything so mundane as the English rugby team. I remember so well before the Romanian match, sitting on the coach alongside Wade Dooley, who was also winning his first cap. Most of the crowd had never heard of his club, Preston Grasshoppers, let alone Dooley himself, and as we drove into the car park, Bob Hesford, the Bristol number eight, was pointing at Dooley and shouting his name out of the window by way of introduction. But on the day we played France in the final match of the 1991 season, our supporters left their cars, their hampers and their vintage wines in droves to welcome us.

The French were also unbeaten. They had played with a panache and enterprise which contrasted sharply with our more prosaic but equally effective style. Their try that day by Philippe Saint-Andre, after eleven minutes, will remain as one of the most gloriously audacious ever scored on the ground. They were worthy opponents, and any side who could beat them could justifiably claim to be in the top bracket. Despite the intense disappointment of Murrayfield, I felt that the last leg of the Grand Slam was a bit like reaching the cup final. Just to get there is a proud achievement. It was an honour and a privilege to have been part of it. But had we lost to Ireland, I honestly don't know how we would have coped, especially those of us who had survived so many losing campaigns.

I don't think that anyone who hasn't been through a championship season can possibly appreciate just how physically and emotionally draining the whole experience is. The hours before kickoff weighed heavily. Some of us had turned up late for the team meeting on the Friday, but Carling sensibly ignored it. 'Get your timing right on the field,' was all he said. Throughout the game we held rigidly to our plan. We probed the weakest areas of the French game with ruthless precision. We bombarded Blanco once more, we hustled Berbizier and we more than matched the intimidatory tactics of the French forwards. The rapier flashed three times and they scored three sumptuous tries. But this was a day for the heavy artillery. Hodgkinson, a model of reliability, kicked four penalties and Rory came good again with another try.

I have known some tense finishes in my time but none more so than that 21-19 win over France. The relief which engulfed us when the final whistle went was indescribable. It was the sweetest of sounds, a sublime moment that is given to very few. It is in the search for that exquisite sensation that we put ourselves through the physical pain and the mental anguish, that we make the sacrifices and that we are ready to commit ourselves to more of the same next season.

I felt that everything we had been through together since Cooke had become manager, the lessons we had extracted from our victories and the many more we had learned from our defeats, had been channelled towards this one goal. But, like the mountaineer, there is always another peak to conquer and that year there were bigger prizes, higher honours to aim for. The World Cup was only six months away, and before that England were scheduled to tour Australia and

Fiji, playing tests in both countries. We were the best in Europe but were we the best in the world? Taken simply on the results of that tour the answer was emphatically no. Three wins, one against Fiji and two in the midweek matches, against four losses, the heaviest being to the Australians, 40-15, was not, on the face of it, the stuff of prospective world champions.

But there were mitigating circumstances. The tour began in late June, two months after the end of our season. Cooke's plan was that we would have a two-month break and then use the tour as a build-up to our preparations for the World Cup, hosted by the four home countries and France in October and November.

There were two events worthy of recall from the tour, one major, the other extremely minor. It was in the test against Fiji that I scored my first try for England. On the scale of brilliance it registered about 0.5, the ball bouncing loose behind the Fijian line and requiring only a pair of hands to touch it down. The hands just happened to be mine. Still, it was reason enough for modest celebration, although our partying had to be toned down after the high jinks of the midweek side. In the early hours of Wednesday morning the Sheraton Hotel at Nadi had been rocking to the sound of the touring minstrels, Ollie Redman on drums, Damian Hopley on trumpet and John Olver on speed. Geoff Cooke had been wakened by the hotel management to put an end to this unholy rumpus but when he stormed into the room he was slightly disarmed by Redman who bellowed over to his fellow ravers, 'Great to see Cookie still up with the lads.' Cooke, whose wife, Sue, had just joined him on tour, was not amused.

There was no cause whatever to celebrate our record defeat by Australia, even though they had given one of the finest displays I have ever seen on a rugby field. Bob Dwyer, the Wallabies coach, later went on record as saying that it was the best eighty minutes of rugby he had witnessed. I remember being interviewed on television at the end of the game and being asked how England could possibly come to terms with a defeat of that magnitude. My immediate response was that we had played very well. The interviewer was clearly perplexed. But in certain areas we had played exceptionally well. Guscott and Carling had ripped through Tim Horan and Jason Little time and again. Our running behind the scrum had been of the highest order and we had scored two well-taken tries. It was up front that we had taken a fearful pounding, especially in the back row, where we had no response to

Willie Ofahengaue, Tim Gavin and Simon Poidevin. On that day at the Sydney Football Stadium were sown the seeds of our downfall in the World Cup final at Twickenham four months later.

The Australian experience proved to me just how far English rugby had fallen behind countries in the southern hemisphere, not so much in playing standards, but in our psychological approach to the game. There is an overwhelming arrogance about the All Blacks and the Springboks, for whom rugby is the means by which they can prove their superiority to the outside world, and the same applies to the Australians, who place success in any sport above almost everything else. England, the European champions, had not yet come to terms with their higher standing in the world rankings. There was still an inbred apprehension when it came to testing ourselves against these sides, who were very often no better than us and in some cases markedly inferior.

That was unquestionably true when we played the opening match of the World Cup against the All Blacks at Twickenham. We had spent three weeks building towards the moment. We had played three warm-up matches, we had devoted every waking hour to thinking about it but, when the time came, we froze. Simple as that. We failed utterly to do ourselves justice. In golfing parlance we got the yips, which was as frustrating for us as it was for our supporters. It was all the more infuriating to discover that the All Blacks were as tentative and unsure of themselves as we were. The only difference was that they made a better job of concealing it. Before the tournament began, an edict had gone out to all the referees that they had to encourage players to stay on their feet, and Jim Fleming, the referee for this match, clearly felt that he had to set an example. His insistence that players remained on their feet and didn't go to ground after a tackle probably affected us more adversely than it did the All Blacks, but that was no excuse for our defeat, nor could it explain our insipid performance.

We hadn't been able to live with the pressure, we weren't the mature rugby nation we thought we were, and when the All Blacks stepped up the pace in the twenty minutes after half time, keeping the ball in hand, moving us around the field, taking quick throw-ins and breaking up the few patchwork patterns we were able to fit together, I knew that we would have to write this one off to experience. We lost 18-12. It could have been more but it should have been different. We were kicking ourselves afterwards for having let slip such a golden opportunity.

It meant that we could afford no more mistakes in the two remaining pool matches against Italy and the United States. Although Cooke made a number of changes, we knew that we must win both handsomely to restore confidence. Richard Hill and I played in all three pool games, which meant that our understudies, Dewi Morris and David Pears, spent the entire competition in a state of restless inactivity which must have been extremely frustrating for them. The World Cup was described as being like a tour at home, but it was nothing like that. There was not the opportunity for all the squad members to play regularly. There was also a great deal of spare time to fill and one of the biggest enemies was monotony. Very wisely the Rugby Football Union had decided that after the pool matches, we should have a weekend break with wives and girlfriends in Jersey. It was an enjoyably relaxing couple of days spent in an agreeable climate and delightful company. The ideal recuperation before turning our minds to the job of playing our quarter-final tie against France in Paris. We had become a close-knit group, the women were part of the team, and it was a pleasant change to see the media switching their attention to them.

Sadly, it was all too short. The tournament rules demanded that we had to travel to Paris on the Monday. Admittedly, there are worse places to spend a week, but we would have preferred to have done our preparatory work in England and travelled to France on the Thursday. There wasn't a player in the squad who didn't harbour the fear, unspoken, of defeat by France. The prospect of losing in Paris on the Saturday and returning to work on the Monday was too hideous to contemplate. Those were negative, private thoughts. Carling and Cooke were interested only in extolling the positive. That week Cooke also had to make one of the most painful decisions of his managerial career, the dropping of Dean Richards.

Ever since his first international, when he had scored two tries, Richards had been a key member of the England side. For someone whose style was so at odds with the textbook coaching of number eight play, he had exerted massive influence not only in Europe, but throughout the world. He was, to my mind, the Lions' best forward in Australia in 1989, despite the fact that it was Mike Teague who had received the accolade of the player of the series. I can think of no more reassuring presence on the field than Richards, and those given the infallibility of hindsight were quick to point to his absence as one of the reasons for our defeat in the final. But what they conveniently chose to forget was the fact that Richards had not been playing well. He had been seriously outplayed in the summer test against the Australians and had been well below his best in the World Cup pool matches. Against the French we knew that we would have to cut down their loose forwards at source. We dared not allow them to gain as much as an inch of momentum, otherwise they would wreak havoc in our defence. Of the many qualities that Richards possessed, advancing nimbly into the tackle was not one of them. Teague and Mickey Skinner, on the other hand, drooled at the prospect of playing such a game. This was what they did best. Not only would they stop the French around the fringes, but, with luck, they would knock them back.

Cooke, as so often, was spot-on with his analysis. It was Skinner's tackle on Marc Cecillon which turned the game England's way. I have seen many important tackles by flankers in my career, and, over the years, no single player has put in more of them than Peter Winterbottom, but few have had a greater impact on a match or a more devastating effect on the opposition than Skinner's crushing demolition of Cecillon. Skinner and the rest of the England pack were more highly motivated for that match than any other I can recall. Our training that week had been physically hard to the point of brutality. After the break in Jersey, Cooke had wanted to restore the mean streak without which we had no chance of survival, so he had ordered a full-blooded contact session on the Wednesday. Richards had already been told of Cooke's decision to drop him and had taken it very well. Nevertheless there was a residue of strong feeling within the squad. The exchanges were fierce and might have resulted in serious injury. I was pole-axed by a punch from John Olver which could have broken my jaw. But it was what we needed to focus our minds on the task ahead.

The next two matches were to be played at a level of commitment none of us had previously experienced. Before the French game two words cropped up time and again. They were discipline and control. Control of the ball, control of ourselves and discipline in all things. The French, we knew, would do everything in their very considerable power to provoke us. They realised that our game was based on order,

Youth Opportunity Scheme. Dad decides to cut down on the farm overheads, and I land my first job.

The Andrew family. Mum, Dad and the brood – David, Jayne, Richard and me.

The proud skipper of the Barnard Castle Under 12s, and the first of countless photographs taken with Rory Underwood (front row, left). Kenneth King (extreme right), a coach of infinite patience and understanding.

One of the very few weddings Sara and I have managed to attend together – our own.

'Heads we bat, tails you field'. I toss, Allan Border calls.

Halcyon days. The free running game adapted by Cambridge which found full expression in the Varsity match of 1984.

Panic attack. My first cap against Romania in 1985 and the opposition haven't left me with many options.

Who says I can't pass? One straight from the coaching manual (circa 1950).

Body language. Every muscle, every nerve in Grant Fox's frame perfectly demonstrate the intense concentration required to be a successful goal kicker.

Above right: Naas Botha may not have been the most naturally gifted of players, but his kicking technique was faultless. Another three points in the bag.

Below left: The Master. Phil Bennett, rugby genius and the inspiration behind a host of aspiring fly halves, myself included.

Below right: Michael Lynagh, as close as they come to being the 'perfect ten', and the outstanding fly half in the modern game.

The departure of Jonathan Davies to the professional code was the most grievous loss to rugby union.

Hugo Porta (above right) played as close to opposition defences as the matador to the bull. A magnificent ambassador for the game.

Balance, grace, timing. John Rutherford had the lot.

Ian McGeechan, the canniest of Scots and the shrewdest of coaches.

'One day a rooster, the next a feather duster.' Alan Jones, (above right) never short of a quote or a quip, experienced the highs and lows during his time as Australian coach, but none could match his intellect or his skill as a motivator.

Straight down the middle. The holy trinity of Geoff Cooke, Roger Uttley and Will Carling who helped steer England to unparalleled success, drive into unfamiliar territory.

on forward power and rigid control. If they could upset that they would irreparably damage our game plan. But after three successive victories against the French we had the beating of them, and well they knew it.

The shelling of Serge Blanco began at approximately one minute past three on the afternoon of Saturday, 19 October 1991. The first two balls I received went straight for him. I can't remember hoisting two more deadly missiles. There was no escape route for him. He was savaged by our pack and rucked out the back in an undignified heap. *C'est magnifique* but, so far as Blanco was concerned, *ce n'est pas la guerre*. His reason seemed to leave him. Skinner and Champ squared up to each other in a macho display of posturing and then Blanco, captaining his country in what was to be his last international appearance, shamefully punched a defenceless Nigel Heslop. Had it been an occasion other than this one he would surely have been sent off. Blanco the beauty had become the beast. He had been unhinged by our tactics and his intemperance quickly spread throughout the side. Still we continued with our target practice. Hill and I had spent every spare moment in training working on our high kicks and now it was paying handsome dividends. But the French were made of sterner stuff than we had thought. They began to cut back our lead, drawing level at 10-10. Then came Skinner's greatest hit. Cecillon was uprooted and the English pack with Brian Moore snarling in triumph swept forward. Jon Webb's penalty minutes later scraped over the bar, then, in the dying seconds, Carling was driven over for a try. As Webb was preparing to take the conversion, Teague shouted over to him, 'Finish 'em off, Webbie.' Only then could we be certain that we had reached the semi-final. That night in Paris we had the mother of all parties.

Paris for a week was one thing; Edinburgh, the scene of our downfall in 1990, was something entirely different. The days leading up to the semi-final against Scotland were among the worst I have spent on the international circuit. Everywhere we went in the city we were subjected to a constant barrage of abuse, some of it good-natured banter but much of it maliciously intended. There was little respite even in our hotel, which was in the city centre. Golf on the magnificent but damnably difficult links at Gullane provided some welcome release and relaxation from the daily diet of taunting and training, and a pub around the corner from the hotel offered us sanctuary in the evenings. Our management gave serious consideration to moving our headquarters out of Edinburgh, but it would have led to complications with the organising committee. It was, therefore, decided to stick it out and, like Cardiff a few months earlier, we were better able to cope with the pressure on match day as a result.

The selectors made one change to the side which had beaten France. It was felt that Simon Halliday would give us more of a physical presence on the wing than Nigel Heslop who was, in any case, still groggy after his contretemps with Blanco. The game was tight, taut and tetchy. Despite the occasion there was none of the atmosphere that had surrounded the Grand Slam match. There was so much to gain, too much to lose. With scores tied at 6-6, Gavin Hastings had a penalty to put the Scots ahead. It wasn't difficult by normal standards, but this was an abnormal situation and he fluffed it. England moved into striking distance and won a five-metre scrum. No part of our game had provoked more argument in team talks than in this particular area of the field. Invariably in such a position the forwards would go for a pushover or attempt a back-row move. Not once, however, during the past three seasons had we ever managed to score from such a manoeuvre. This was in contrast to the Australians who, the previous summer, had managed three tries in one match alone from back-row moves. But there was to be no arguing with our pack on this occasion. They called a back-row move and Teague, going on a lateral run, was brought down. At least we had advanced closer to the posts, if not to the Scottish line, and we had retained the put-in to the scrummage. The ball came back perfectly from Hill and, from close range, I dropped the goal which effectively ended the attritional battle and put us into the final. Relief, as always on such occasions, comes far in advance of the joy of having won and the realisation of the achievement, but the train journey south the following day in the company of our delirious supporters was one that none of us will ever forget.

We were heading for Belton Woods, a luxurious hotel near Grantham where, once again, we were to meet up with our wives, families and girlfriends. Sara had been at Murrayfield and had flown to London on the Sunday morning to collect little Emily and bring her up to the hotel. It was as if we had won the cup itself. Everywhere we went we were fêted, we were congratulated. We couldn't have cared less at that stage who we were going to play in the final. Australia and New Zealand were contesting the other semi-final at Lansdowne Road that afternoon and we arrived at out hotel just in time to watch it on television. Personally, I wanted the All Blacks to win so that we could show our supporters how well we really could play against them. Given a second crack I knew without the slightest doubt that we would beat them. But they were never in with a chance against the inspired Australians who, at times in the first half, were awesome in their forward control and in the boldness of their backs. It was Campese's match. He mesmerised the All Blacks' defence, making the impossible seem commonplace. He scored one try and, with outrageous effrontery, set up another for Tim Horan. Few have Campese's capacity to thrill and to infuriate in equal measure. Having helped win the match for Australia he then spent most of the following week criticising our style and contemptuously dismissing our chances. 'The convicts will smash the toffs,' was one of his least inflammatory remarks.

The popular view is that England were talked out of winning the World Cup by the press and by the Australians. The story goes that we were so goaded by comments about 'boring England' that we made the decision to play a more expansive game in the final. The truth of the matter is that there were no outside pressures. The tactical shift was made by our coaches with the full agreement of the squad, and the seeds of change had been sown the previous summer in Australia. Admittedly, Sydney in July cannot accurately be compared to Twickenham in November, and the view during the summer that our forwards would not be strong enough to hold the Wallabies made little sense in the light of their performance throughout the World Cup. No matter, the decision was taken to change the emphasis towards a more fluid game. It was a unanimous decision, one collectively approved by every member of the team. If there were dissenting voices, they were not heard during any of the policy discussions before the final. Several players have since expressed their displeasure with our tactics on the day, but not one of them stood up to offer their opinions at the time.

Of greater concern to Cooke and Uttley in the days before the final was our attitude. Sara had remarked at Belton that she felt there was too much celebration of what we had achieved and too little concentration on what still had to be done. The Australians had come with no thoughts other than to be crowned as world champions, but perhaps we had set our sights a notch or two lower. The satisfaction of getting so close to the summit had perhaps blinded us to the very real prospect of reaching the pinnacle itself.

The pre-match rituals were much the same as for any other international. We went on to the field to sniff the air. On these occasions the kickers tend to toss up blades of grass more from nervous habit than to gauge the strength of the wind. The Australians were on the pitch at the same time, which was annoying. Traditionally, the forwards steadfastly refuse to acknowledge each other's presence, but on our way back to the dressing room I caught Michael Lynagh's eye and we nodded solemnly to each other. We had become good friends and there is no finer ambassador for his sport. Back in the dressing room it was the usual scene. Rory, still in his blazer and as laid-back as ever, was in a corner reading the match programme. Richard Hill and I started to change. We always liked to have a ten-minute session kicking the ball to each other. Jon Webb was another who wanted to get the feel of the ball before going out. And then there was the customary queue awaiting Kevin Murphy's attentions. He worked overtime on such occasions, applying strapping or soothing hands to the tender areas, real or imagined.

There was also an illegal immigrant in our midst, Ian O'Donoghue, the ITV cameraman who had been with us throughout the tournament. He was well respected and had gained the confidence of the players. A request had been made by ITV, the host broadcaster, to the Rugby Football Union to have a camera in the England dressing room after the match, but this had been flatly refused by Dudley Wood, the RFU secretary. But the players felt that such a historic occasion should be captured for the television viewers and we conspired to smuggle O'Donoghue in through the security screen, wearing England kit, with his camera concealed in a holdall. It worked perfectly. O'Donoghue remained hidden in the dressing room during the match and was ready waiting for us when we returned approximately an hour and a half later.

It was perhaps the most important ninety minutes of our lives. We walked out for the gladiatorial combat as we had done so many times before, down the ramp, up the steps and on to the pitch. The pre-match formalities were even more formal than usual in the presence of the Queen. There were sixty thousand spectators in the ground and millions unseen around the world watching on television. The ceremonial, the splendour of the occasion, the anticipation of the event were all a cut above the game itself. Australia won, not through the brilliance of their loudly heralded attack, but because of the quality of their defence. Their try, from a maul following a line-out, was hardly a work of art and the brightest moments of enterprise came from England. Our forwards quickened the pace, our backs began to create space and suddenly the Wallabies looked vulnerable. 'Why in heaven's name did England not change tack and return to the tactics which had got them to the final?' The question has been asked so often. The answer, quite simply, is that we didn't feel the need to change.

The Australians were fighting for their lives and who is to say that if we had returned to our old ways we would have been any more successful? We had not, in any case, gone that far off piste. We were still recognisable as the team which had won the Grand Slam a few months earlier. With the score at 12-6 Guscott broke gloriously only to be cut down by Nick Farr-Jones in a game- and championship-winning tackle.

It was all over, almost as soon as it had started, but for the Australians those closing moments must have seemed endless. Within minutes of our return to the dressing room and the arrival of the Prime Minister, John Major, to meet us, the television pictures were being beamed to the world and to the committee room at Twickenham. Dudley Wood was apoplectic with rage when he saw them. But the scenes made for great television and, despite the result, the England dressing room in the aftermath of the most important game in the nation's rugby history was not the worst place on earth to be.

CHAPTER 6

French Lessons

For the players, the 1991 World Cup had been an unqualified success. Doubts were expressed over the administration of the tournament and there was disappointment, dismay in some quarters, that the financial profits had fallen so far below expectation. The first casualty of that failure was the development of the game among the emerging countries. Yet it was the younger rugby-playing nations who had contributed so significantly to the richness of the event. Western Samoa and Canada, in their own very individual ways, reached the last eight. Both learned from their experiences but they also taught the other countries a thing or two. It was a measure of the Samoans' rising status that the Scots were so relieved to have beaten them in the quarter-finals. After that tie, John Jeffrey said it was one of the hardest matches he had ever played. The Canadians, for their part, had made the All Blacks fight every inch of the way. The Italians, the Japanese, the Argentinians and all the other participating countries had contributed to a spectacle for which, as Bob Dwyer so aptly remarked afterwards, 'the world had stood still'.

The impact was incredible. The television coverage ensured that the game spread far beyond the rugby community. The England players were, for the first time, household names. It was impossible to walk down a main street in London without being recognised. That had never happend in all the time I had played for England. It was not easy to come to terms with. Still less was it easy to come back down to earth when it was all over. Yesterday the world, tomorrow the office.

I would have to reintroduce myself to my colleagues on Monday. One thing was sure, business wasn't getting any better. The recession in the property market, which had begun to bite the previous year, had reached rock bottom. I was too young, surely, to be going through the male menopause, but for some time I had felt unsettled. I was getting itchy feet. It was time for a change and Sara felt the same way. Since Emily's arrival our lives had altered appreciably. It baffles me when couples say that parenthood changes nothing. Sara had just been promoted to the job she had spent years working towards, as a product manager in pharmaceuticals, when she became pregnant. So that was the end of that. My life away from home continued much as before. Work, training and playing for Wasps, work, training and playing for London, work, training and playing for England. It was no different from last year and no different from the year before that. There was a repetitiveness about it which was becoming monotonous. I was twenty-nine and realised that if we as a family were to consider making a major change in our lives, this was the time to do it. Sara agreed.

For some while I had been drawn to the idea of playing rugby in France. I had played for England in Paris and had gone with Wasps to the south-west of the country on the club's pre-season tour. Since 1987, when they went to Dax, Wasps had been crossing the Channel prior to the start of the domestic season. They had made their base at Saint-Jean-de-Luz, near Biarritz. I always looked forward to those expeditions and thoroughly enjoyed the rugby. Without realising it, I had become a Francophile. There were other reasons for my fascination with French rugby. During England's training week in Portugal in 1989, Pierre Villepreux, the great French full back of the sixties and seventies and one of the world's most knowledgeable coaches, came at the behest of Don Rutherford to assist in the coaching. It was a revelation to hear him talk and to listen to his theories on rugby. He should, of course, have been the national coach in France, but had never found favour with Albert Ferrasse, the dictatorial president of the French Federation. France's loss was on this occasion our gain and Ferrasse was said to be furious. Villepreux would never be given the chance to take charge of the national side but he did coach Toulouse, along with the former international flank forward Jean-Claude Skrela.

I had kept in touch with Villepreux since Portugal and it was on an impulse in the February of 1991 that I phoned him to ask about the possibility of coming over to play for Toulouse. My firm in London had a sister company, Jean Thouard, who had offices throughout France. The recommendation from London was that if I wanted to proceed with the idea, I should go to Paris, but Sara and I were determined to break the mould and head for the provinces. Going from London to Paris would be trading one capital city for another. Besides, I wanted to play for Toulouse where, by good fortune, Jean Thouard had a base. The plan was that I would spend a couple of years in Toulouse and then move to Paris for another two years. After that we would consider our position, but at this stage Sara and I regarded it very much as a long-term venture.

I fully realised that by playing in France, out of the selectorial eye, I might be jeopardising my prospects of being picked for England, but it was a chance I was prepared to take. It was a major decision in our lives, however, and I needed some reassurance that I was doing the right thing. I had a responsibility to Sara and to Emily and needed to be convinced that I was not acting selfishly on some reckless whim. I was invited to go over to meet the president and the officials of Toulouse in May, on the weekend when the club were playing in the semi-final of the National Championship against Racing Club. As always at this stage of the competition, the matches were played on neutral territory, and the venue for this one was Bordeaux. The next day Bègles and Béziers were to play in the other semi-final at Toulouse.

I arrived at Bordeaux airport to be met by club officials. We made straight for a café and more introductions. But the rugby world can be a dangerously small place. The first two people I saw in the café were Clem Thomas, the *Observer*'s rugby correspondent, and his chum Alan Watkins, greatly respected as a political writer who also indulges his passion for rugby with a weekly newspaper column. Thomas was agog to know what I was doing in Bordeaux. He quickly put two and two together and was just about to come up with the right answer when I produced from nowhere the inspired deception that I was across covering both matches for *The Times*, for whom I was contracted to write the occasional article. That seemed to satisfy the investigative streak in both their natures, although Thomas subsequently told me that he had a pretty good idea all along what was happening. But at least he did the decent thing and kept it to himself. Any announcement at that time would have been extremely embarrassing.

The semi-final at Bordeaux was a splendid occasion. The French club championship is quite unique. There is fervour, passion and fun, all the clamour and colour of a football crowd but without the menace.

Toulouse won 13-12 with a drop goal in the last minute of the game. All the way back on the road to Toulouse, cars were passing, horns hooting, black and red scarves streaming out of the windows. It was impossible not to be swept up in the joyous rapture of the day. That evening before dinner, I walked out of my hotel into the city square. It was still hot and people were sitting outside the cafés and bars. This, I thought, is where I want to spend the next part of my life with Sara and Emily.

There were still plans to be made and negotiations to be completed. First I had to tell Wasps. Clem Thomas might be able to keep a secret but I knew plenty of other journalists who would spill the beans once they got a sniff of the story, and I certainly didn't want my club to get first news of my intentions from the papers. Furthermore, there was the situation at Toulouse, which had been complicated by the recent arrival of Christophe Deylaud, an international fly half cum centre from Toulon. The club's regular fly half, Philippe Rougé-Thomas, who had also been capped by France, was something of a folk hero in the town. He had played in the championship final that year when Toulouse lost to Bègles. It was a sensitive situation requiring tact and diplomacy. Toulouse, like most of the other major clubs in France, tended to rely on home-based talent. Seldom were they attracted by players from overseas, and they had gone to great lengths to make it known that if I came to Toulouse, it would be the result of a career move in business, not in rugby.

I received a frosty reception when I walked into the dressing room to meet my new team-mates for the first time. I had finally sorted out the business side of the move on the day before England played France in the World Cup quarter-final in Paris. It was agreed that I would start work in Toulouse at the beginning of January 1992. From first to last the negotiations had taken nearly six months and there were newspaper articles on both sides of the Channel on the subject of my impending move. The comments in France were less than complimentary. I would not, they said, be welcome at the club. What did a side with two international fly halves want with another one from England? It hadn't exactly helped my cause that England had beaten France in the World Cup or that we hadn't lost to them since 1988.

It was into this hostile environment that three tired and lonely creatures arrived on a dank Sunday night in January. The airport at

Toulouse was fog-bound and our flight had been diverted to Lourdes. A two-and-a-half-hour bus journey in a strange country with an increasingly fractious infant is one of life's more dispiriting experiences. Temporary accommodation had been arranged for us near the city centre in a modest one-bedroomed flat. Just how modest we were to discover later that night. We were awakened in the early hours by music blasting out from the neighbouring apartment. It was being played by an inebriated long-distance lorry driver who, I later discovered, had lost his wife and three-year-old son in a car accident some weeks previously. Whenever he came back from his tour of duty on the French highways he drank himself into oblivion in order to try to forget his grief. Unfortunately, he also found solace in playing music very loud. One night I sat up with him for three hours as this shattered soul poured out his heart. It was impossible not to feel sorry for him but we were greatly relieved when the time came, six weeks later, to move into a house on the outskirts of the city. Since then, whenever I see a lorry with French number plates, I give it a very wide berth.

Before we left England, Sara and I organised French lessons, which we continued once we were in Toulouse. But so thick is the accent in that part of the world that it was initially very difficult to understand anything of what was said. This put me at a disadvantage with the players, a number of whom were highly suspicious of me in the first place. I had gone over to play in a reserve team game in December in order to comply with the registration requirements. The game was on the Saturday and I was introduced to members of the first team squad at training on the Friday night. It was an experience I would never like to repeat. I have never felt more ill at ease. One or two of the players, like Eric Bonneval, the wing, and the second row, Jean-Marie Cadieu, who had played against us in the World Cup, I already knew. But many of them were supporters of Rougé-Thomas, despite the fact that he was extremely injury-prone and, at thirty-two, getting very close to the end of his playing career. I also knew Skrela, the coach, but to my dismay I discovered that Villepreux had left for the Italian club Treviso on a three-year coaching contract. I had, therefore, lost one of my staunchest allies. His successor as the backs' coach was Christian Gajan, a Rougé-Thomas man, who played a wily political game.

It was with the emerging second team, known as the Espoirs, that I found my niche and through them that I began to earn the respect of the senior players. Here I was, a seasoned international player with nearly fifty caps and a Lions tour, having to prove myself all over again. It was a huge challenge but one which I relished. Because of my involvement with England through the Five Nations Championship, I was seldom available for the club, which meant that for the first two months I played mostly second-team rugby. Every other week, when there was an international match, Sara, Emily and I would travel back to England. It was not the ideal way of building up a relationship with my French playing colleagues, but again it was all part of the challenge. The training, four times a week, was incredibly intense. The practice games between first and second teams were red-blooded affairs where no quarter was given or asked. It was in practice that I discovered how well Rougé-Thomas could tackle. It was some of the hardest hitting I had ever taken. So hot-tempered did these contests sometimes become that it was not uncommon for Skrela to send players off.

If nothing else it kept me fit and sharp for the International Championship in which England were attempting a second successive Grand Slam, a feat last achieved by an England side in 1923–24. With the exception of Paul Ackford, who had decided to retire, the World Cup team had remained intact. We also had a new coach, Dick Best, in succession to Roger Uttley who had announced his decision to go at the end of the World Cup. He had done a magnificent job in his four years with the side. He had helped instil confidence and self-belief in players who had known only frustration and defeat with England. He took us back to basics and restored the pride in playing for our country. Beyond that he recognised that he could do no more, and wisely he went out at the top.

The team that Best inherited was clearly the one that would battle through the forthcoming series. The players were fit, and thanks to the World Cup they knew each other as well as any club combination. There was also a large residue of confidence built up from our performances in the World Cup which the other countries did not have. The Scots, who had more than fulfilled their potential in the tournament, had since lost a number of key players, including John Jeffrey and Finlay Calder. Without them they were a spent force in the Five Nations Championship. On the opening Saturday of the series, England went to Murrayfield, overcame the embarrassment of conceding a pushover try early in the game and won effortlessly 25-7. It was at this point that we realised there would be none of the pressure which had accompanied our forced march to the

Grand Slam the previous season. We might actually start to enjoy our matches. Martin Bayfield had moved seamlessly into Ackford's place in the second row and Dewi Morris had replaced Richard Hill at scrum half. This was another hard decision for Geoff Cooke to have to make. Hill had played in all six World Cup matches with his customary combativeness. But he had lost his edge in the intervening weeks and Cooke, for whom loyalty was important but never to the extent that it clouded his judgement, dropped him. Ireland went the way of Scotland, only more so, 38-9, and then, once again, it was France in Paris, just four months after our tumultuous meeting in the World Cup.

As something of a Trojan horse I was much in demand in the weeks leading up to the match. Television crews came from all over France and from the UK. I was filmed walking in the square, drinking in the clubhouse, and talking with anyone who would stop for long enough. On one occasion the producer wheeled out the city elders and filmed me playing a game of boules with them. Quite what those gnarled old veterans thought of it all I'm not sure, but they sucked on their pipes, nodded sagely and entered into the spirit of things. Everyone in and around Toulouse ventured an opinion on the game. The coverage was well over the top, but the interest in rugby in that part of France is almost without parallel anywhere in the world. If you were to draw a line from Bordeaux to Nice, the road signs along the route read like a directory of rugby – Toulon, Narbonne, Perpignan, Dax, Bayonne, Pau, Auch, Castres and so on. Every town large and small has its rugby club.

Toulouse lies in the heart of this rugby country. The players at the club are local celebrities, instantly recognised wherever they go. The rugby supporters are far more knowledgeable about the game and its characters than they are in England. And they are more passionate about it. Four months on from the World Cup and there was still a hangover from the quarter-final defeat. Despite the fact that I was now playing regularly for the club and was just beginning to make an impression with the locals, I still had not been forgiven for my part in that defeat. Another win for England could make life very difficult.

Three things worked in my favour for this particular match. The first was that Jean-Marie Cadieu, the Toulouse lock, who had played in the World Cup, was left out of the French side. There was no love lost between Toulouse and the French Federation. Jean Fabre, the millionaire businessman associated with the club, had been favourite to succeed Albert Ferrasse as president of the FFR, but in a typical piece of machiavellian trading had been outvoted. The politics of French rugby make the Borgias seem like the Swiss Family Robinson. The consistent dismissal of Villepreux, with his glaringly obvious claims to be the national coach, was another reason for the club's contempt for the governing body, added to which they believed that there was a selectorial conspiracy against them when it came to picking players for the national side. The omission of Cadieu offered further proof of that, and so there were probably as many at the club praying that France would lose as there were hoping that England wouldn't extend what was becoming an impressive run of victories. Four in a row, and two of them at Parc des Princes where Scotland and Ireland hadn't won since rugby was first played on the ground twenty years previously, and where Wales had last won in 1975. The third reason for my escape from the French equivalent of being sent to Coventry was that I played for only thirty minutes of the match before leaving the field with a gash above the eye which required six stitches. When I left, England were losing 4-3. When the final whistle blew against the remnants of the shambolic French side, England had won 31-13. I could justifiably argue, therefore, that I had done my best for France!

In fact the only enemy within the French camp that day was the Gallic temperament which surfaced in all its uncontrolled fury and ruined any chance of victory. All resistance crumbled after the captain, Philippe Sella, left the field injured. Shortly afterwards there was a moment of high farce when Jean–Luc Sadourny and Alain Penaud collided, and England raced upfield to score. The French front row, who had been under intense pressure from the very first scrummage and whose tolerance threshold was closer to their feet than to what passed for their brains, snapped. The red mists came down and Vincent Moscato and Gregoire Lascubé were sent off by the Irish referee Stephen Hilditch, a brave man indeed. Even after their dismissal, Jean-François Tordo was running wild, a loose cannon with fists and boots thrashing out indiscriminately. Most of it was aimed at Brian Moore, who has much the same effect on French forwards as a red rag does on a bull.

At least something constructive was to emerge from the debris of what had been a shameful French display. I appeared on a television programme the following Monday with Fabien Galthié and Alain

Penaud, the French half backs. The topic of the debate was the current state of the game in France and the attitude of the players. Up until that match everybody had been out of step but the French. There were excuses made about the referees and about the opposition and there was even talk of an Anglo-Saxon conspiracy. At no time was there a moment's thought given to the possibility that the fault might lie with the French themselves. Even after such a short spell of involvement with French rugby it was easy to see that one of the principal causes of their indiscipline was the standard of refereeing in club matches. Players were allowed to get away with behaviour which was totally unacceptable and which was certain to be punished by referees of international standing.

There was also the much more complex problem of the French temperament. The popular misconception of rugby in France is that every game ends up in a free-for-all. That is not so. Ninety per cent of the games in which I played were completed without incident. They were physically hard but in the vast majority of cases very fair. It is the rogue ten per cent, however, which tarnish the game's image. The problem is that when trouble erupts, it escalates. Warning by the referees, dismissal of players, have not the slightest effect. Moreover, it is possible to tell almost from the kickoff whether or not the game is going to be a violent one. It is part of the French character and, like the weather, it will always be with them.

Pierre Berbizier, who succeeded the disgraced Daniel Dubroca as national coach, is a strict disciplinarian, as is Bernard Lapasset, the president of the French Federation, but the problem will exist for as long as it remains rooted in the French character. It is that same temperament, of course, which produces the gloriously liberated back play which is their trademark, and the breathtaking sleight of hand of their forwards. Once French sides are allowed to establish their supremacy they are virtually unbeatable and there is no more thrilling sight in rugby. David Berty, the Toulouse wing who played for France, was the embodiment of the good and the bad in their game. He would score some superlative tries with matchless individual brilliance. He would also be prone to monumental aberrations in which he would field the ball behind his own line and, instead of touching down for a drop-out, would attempt to beat the four or five opponents in front of him. As often as not he would lose the ball and the opposition would score. Afterwards he would be full of remorse, but for the life of him he was powerless to explain why he did it. So often I would be standing deep in defence shouting '*Pas de connerie!*' – which, politely translated, means 'For God's sake don't do anything stupid' – that it became a standing joke at the club. But it was infuriating to see so many good players needlessly committing so many silly mistakes.

In the midst of this the Five Nations Championship was building to its climax. England stood one game away from a second successive Grand Slam but unlike the previous season, when every match seemed to go down to the wire, there was an overwhelming confidence within the side that we would win the Welsh game as comfortably as we had won the others. The World Cup had had its effect on the other countries, no doubt about that. Scotland had lost players, Ireland had lost the impetus they had found in their spectacular quarter-final against Australia and the French had lost heart. Wales had been losing just about everything. Their World Cup had been yet another gloomy setback in the series of disasters which had befallen them in the past eighteen months. They had failed to get beyond the pool stage of the tournament and would have to prequalify for the next event in four years' time. We always knew it was a game we were going to win, the only question was by how much.

The margin of our victory by 24-0 would have been a pipe dream in years gone by but it was probably our most disappointing performance of the season. We so badly wanted to put on a show for our supporters but we were frustrated by the Welsh tactics of damage limitation and we could never scale the heights we reached against Ireland and France. In the end Wales were delighted with the result and we were rather less overjoyed than we should have been to be only the third side in history to have won back-to-back Grand Slams.

Part of our irritation lay in the fact that we had been unable to engineer a try for Dewi Morris or Rory Underwood. Both had scored tries in each one of the three previous Championship matches and we were keen for one or the other, preferably both, to join an élite band of players who had achieved the feat of scoring a try in all four matches. I was especially keen for Rory to do it in what we thought was going to be his last international. Earlier in the season he had announced that he would retire from rugby at the end of that campaign. He was the longest-serving player in the side, after Peter Winterbottom, was England's most capped player, having won his first cap against France in 1984, and was, by a comfortable margin, the leading try scorer in

England's history. His was a rare talent and I for one would miss his companionship in the national side. It might be a slight overstatement to say that I owed my life to him but I certainly owed him my lasting gratitude. It was during my first week at Barnard Castle School, I was eleven years of age and I couldn't swim. I was standing by the pool thinking up all sorts of excuses for not getting wet when a senior boy pushed me into the deep end. It was as I was coming up for the second time and showing very obvious signs of distress that Rory dived in and fished me out. It was our first meeting and was the start of an enduring friendship. I told that story on television when Rory was the subject of a *This is Your Life* programme. He had been ambushed by Michael Aspel and a few of the England players dressed up as firemen when he had come in to land at his RAF base at Wyton after an exercise. It was, we all thought, a fitting tribute for Rory's farewell. What we didn't know was that he would be back in the fold within a matter of months.

The Grand Slam had been won but my season wasn't over. Far from it. Toulouse had reached the quarter-finals of the club championship with a victory over Tordo's club, Nice. By this time I had settled into the first team at fly half, having finally seen off Rougé-Thomas, and Christophe Deylaud was switched to centre. But the side was inconsistent and in the next round we lost to Dax. It was the most appalling display of refereeing I have ever seen, and it prompted an official protest from Toulouse. Before the game there had been clubhouse rumours of impropriety. The referee had been overheard saying that Toulouse would get no further in the competition. The longer one stayed in France the more accustomed one grew to such talk, but on this occasion there seemed very good grounds for believing that the official had been well and truly nobbled. We were 18-3 up at half time but lost 24-18, with Thierry Lacroix kicking six penalty goals and Lescarboura dropping a goal. Hardly ever were we able to cross the halfway line in the second half, and on the few occasions when we did – and the even rarer occasions when we were awarded a penalty within sight of goal – I discovered to my disgust that my kicking form had deserted me.

Because I had played so few first-team games I was still eligible to play for the second team in their championship. They were much more successful. The final against Perpignan was played at Quillan, a small town halfway up the Pyrenees and roughly equidistant between

Toulouse and Perpignan. There was a volatile crowd of five thousand packed into a tiny ground, and surprise, surprise, two players were sent off. But it was a marvellous occasion which went into extra time before Toulouse returned home with the trophy.

By now it was well into June. I had played rugby without a break for twelve months. My travels had taken me to Australia and Fiji, through a Five Nations Championship and all the way to a World Cup final. Looking back, the satisfaction had been enormous, not least for the fact that I had come through my ordeal by examination at Toulouse. Rougé-Thomas had conceded defeat and I was now the number one fly half at the club. Already I was looking forward to the next season. Sara and I had decided that we would extend our sojourn in France.

We were beginning to make friends but, more importantly, we had been able to enjoy each other's company, a luxury seldom granted to us when I had been working and playing in England. We had many wonderful family weekends, travelling sometimes to the Mediterranean coast and on other occasions to Biarritz on the Atlantic side. Sometimes we would drive up into the Pyrenees or inland to the Dordogne. And Toulouse itself was a city of endless fascination. With the largest university outside Paris it was a lively, vibrant place. We were so taken with it that we put down a deposit on a house. But in the forthcoming weeks, events were to change dramatically.

I had been vaguely aware of problems in the Toulouse office. Business was flat. France was by now in the midst of the recession which had held the British economy in its grip for the last two years, and there were hints coming from London that the French sister company might be taken over or, even worse, shut down. I rapidly came to the conclusion that if the ship was sinking I didn't want to be standing on the bridge. There were other clouds on the horizon. There was an attempted coup at the club, led by the French flank forward Karl Janik who had as one of his lieutenants my old friend Rougé-Thomas. The president was forced out and with him went several of the club's sponsors. Financial difficulties loomed as a result of the administrative instability and although I felt my own position on the field was secure, it was unsettling to say the least. To stay would be too much of a risk and so, at the end of October 1992, just ten months after leaving, the family returned to London, and I reappeared, boots in hand, on Wasps' doorstep.

CHAPTER 7

Building the Pyramid

I had joined Wasps in the 1986-87 season after returning from Australia. My career move had taken me from Nottingham to London, and Wasps were the obvious choice. The club had an impressive pool of players and had opened up a productive channel of communication with Cambridge University. Simon Smith, Kevin Simms and Mark Bailey, with whom I had played in my university days, were already at the club and I was looking forward to renewing my association with them. Wasps had a reputation for playing the kind of rugby I enjoyed, besides which they were similar in many ways to my previous club, Nottingham. Neither could be described as glamorous in the way that Leicester, Bath and Harlequins were, but both were efficiently run, well-coached clubs with enough good players to encourage optimism for the future. In the seventies, Wasps had been the poor relations of London rugby. They were languishing in the shadow of Harlequins, Richmond, Rosslyn Park, Saracens and Blackheath. Against these clubs, Wasps held little appeal for players coming to work in the capital. But then came the Cambridge connection, which coincided with the arrival of high-profile players like Roger Uttley, who had taken a teaching post at Harrow School, Nigel Melville and Maurice Colclough. Those were the days before the establishment of a league structure when club fixtures were based on historical associations. But the wind of change was beginning to blow through the game and the more far-sighted clubs were preparing for the day when that change would come. Wasps were fortunate in having members like Peter Yarranton and Alan Black whose positions within the Rugby Football Union gave them early warning of developments in the game.

77

Wasps, like Nottingham, made a little go a long way. Geographically they were in the middle of nowhere. There was no identity with the local community and precious little support. Nor were Wasps financially strong enough to offer incentives to top players. That they had managed to survive was due to the sheer weight of numbers coming to London and the fact that supply so far outstripped demand. They couldn't all go to Harlequins. There was also a social camaraderie that few other clubs could match. This fostered a loyalty which, I believe, is second to none and which has become an increasingly precious commodity. Very few players have left Wasps for reasons other than business commitments.

The key to the club's success in future, of course, would be how well they could adapt to the changing world of rugby and in this, Wasps were better off than most. After the lean years through the seventies they just happened to be at the very top of their cycle when the leagues were instituted in 1987. Again there were similarities with Nottingham in the aggressiveness of their player recruitment. In my final year at Cambridge I had been approached by Alan Davies, the Nottingham coach, after our game against the club. Richard Moon and Andy Martin were with me, and Davies talked persuasively about the advantages of joining Nottingham after we left university. There were no inducements other than the benefits of quality coaching and mixing in the company of some outstanding players like Brian Moore, Peter Cook, Simon Hodgkinson, the Holdstock brothers and Neil Mantell. The three of us joined up without hesitation. Wasps offered similar attractions. Above all, they needed a fly half since the departure of Gareth Rees. Rees, who had joined the club as a schoolboy at Harrow, had played in the cup final against Bath the previous season but had since returned to Canada. Wasps' first appearance in the final in 1986 had signalled their arrival in the top flight of clubs, but without a competitive league system at that time, the route to higher things lay not with the clubs, but through the counties and the divisions.

I had first moved on to the county ladder as an undergraduate at Cambridge and had captained Yorkshire at under-21 level. This was in the days before the reintroduction of the Divisional Championship, when the power base of the English game was county led. It was well supported and traditionally strong in Yorkshire, Lancashire, Warwickshire, Gloucestershire and Cornwall. London counties like

Middlesex and Surrey were still influential and to them could now be added Kent and, in the south-west of England, Somerset, who were starting to benefit from the emergence of Bath as a force in club rugby. Only in Leicestershire did the county play second fiddle to the club. Leicester were powerful enough in their own right to bypass the established route to national selection, but elsewhere the County Championship stood unrivalled as the stage for national recognition and, notwithstanding Leicester's independence, it remained unchallenged as the country's premier domestic competition.

Some of the most enjoyable rugby of my career was played with Yorkshire. The matches were big occasions for some of the lesser lights from smaller clubs and provided a good day out for the army of officials. One of my earliest recollections of an away day was playing for Yorkshire against Somerset. We stayed overnight in Gloucester, and there were so many alickadoos in our party that the players had to stand in the bus going to the match. Yorkshire's game was based out of necessity on running rugby. We didn't have the tight forwards to compete with the big guns of Lancashire and Gloucestershire, but we had an outstanding back row with Peter Winterbottom and Peter Buckton, and top-class backs in Nigel Melville, Bryan Barley, Mike Harrison and Rory Underwood. Our minds were uncluttered by theory, our game simple and uninhibited. Sometimes it failed, more often it was a spectacular success, as it was when we annihilated Lancashire 39-10 at Headingly in 1984. That game, in which I kicked nine goals from ten attempts, together with my performances in the Varsity Match and for the North against the Australians and the Romanians in the same season, won me selection for England.

There is no way nowadays that a player would be assessed for international selection on the strength of four games. The establishment of the league and the reintroduction of the Divisional Championship have changed that. It was the success of the combined regional sides against touring teams which prompted the resurrection of the divisional system, which had been prematurely discarded after a brief experiment some years previously. The inspiration for the divisional concept had come from that extraordinary day at Otley in 1979 when the North had triumphed over Graham Mourie's All Blacks. The North's collective power and influence, which was so totally disproportionate to the standards of rugby played at club level in the region, was hard to fathom. With Yorkshire and Lancashire supplying the bulk of the side, identification of talent was a relatively straightforward task. The few good players were too thinly spread over too many clubs but, perversely, that simplified the process of representative selection. The North had a unity and sense of purpose and pride which the other divisional sides lacked. The players in the south-west, for example, who were selected primarily from three clubs, Bath, Bristol and Gloucester, initially considered it much more important to play for their clubs than for the division. That was never the case in the north, where as many as fourteen clubs could contribute players to the representative side, and felt honoured to do so.

I was, and until very recently have remained, a fervent supporter of the Divisional Championship. By lifting players out of their cosy club environment and requiring them to play in a series of competitive games at a standard higher than they were accustomed to, the selectors were able to make a much more accurate judgement of an individual's strengths and weaknesses, both physically and mentally. Those who decry the divisional concept forget that in the days before the leagues, the identification of players of international calibre tended to be a lottery. In its early years, the Divisional Championship helped overcome that problem and also reduced the likelihood of any repetition of the selectorial aberrations of the past, when success at club level was taken as a yardstick for a player's ability to perform for his country. A disastrous precedent had been set by England when they picked too many Bath players, and was followed some years later by the Welsh who were beguiled by Neath's success in domestic competition. Poor players can very often flourish playing week in week out alongside better players in a successful club side, but their shortcomings will be cruelly exposed at international level. Yet players who performed consistently well in unsuccessful sides were often overlooked. The Divisional Championship therefore enabled the selectors to make their assessments on the much sounder principles of common purpose and equal opportunity.

English rugby not only required a pyramid to ensure that the best players got to the top but it also had to be certain that those players who came to the surface were the best available. The Varsity Match plus the two or three representative games which had propelled me into the England side were no longer sufficient grounds for selection in a game which was changing faster than most people realised.

A national selection panel comprising six or seven selectors from different parts of the country, all with different priorities and basing their judgements on vastly different standards of play, was archaic and inoperable. The incompetence of the system was highlighted in an eighteen-month period between 1984 and 1985 when something like fifty-five players represented England. For the first six or seven years after its re-emergence, the Divisional Championship proved an invaluable aid in the selection of the national side. Geoff Cooke, in part because as a northerner he appreciated the importance of the concept, but mainly because he recognised that there was no alternative, was totally committed to the competition. Indeed, had he got his way, he would have extended it, but the popularity and the influence of the leagues prevented any such notion from coming to fruition. The increase in the number of touring sides to Britain has been one of the main justifications for the continued existence of the divisions, and has ultimately been the most compelling reason for not disbanding them. But the format, the lack of public support and the promotional shortcomings of the Divisional Championship inevitably mean that sooner or later it must be overtaken by events, and no single event has been more important in the advance of England as a rugby power than the establishment of the league structure.

The leagues have changed the face of the game in England and have irreversibly altered its course. Few could have realised the impact they would have when they were set up in the 1987–88 season. Such was the lack of organisation and preparation in those early days that there were no scheduled weeks set aside for league matches. Clubs would simply play for league points when they happened to come up against each other in their existing fixtures, most of which had been established since the year dot. It was all extremely informal but even then the difference for the players was astonishing. There was a sense of anticipation, a buzz of excitement and an urgency on the field for a league game which could never be recreated in friendly matches. Nor could the non-competitive games put bums on seats in the way that league matches did, with the result that friendlies became meaningless contests, unloved by players and club treasurers alike. One by one the traditional fixtures were killed off.

Within three years the ball which the Rugby Football Union had sent rolling gently down the slope had gathered an irresistible momentum. Some famous old clubs, run by dinosaurs who either didn't see the need for change or else wanted no part of it, went down. Others, like Northampton, required a revolution to remain in the top stream. Ambition, resources, facilities and money became the key words. Hon. secs. were replaced by chief execs. It is pointless for the RFU to hold up their hands in horror and complain about the game in England going professional when they were the very instruments of that change. By instituting a competitive structure they encouraged competition in which, by definition, some will win, some will lose. The problem is that it is not just points that are at stake. There is now enormous financial pressure on clubs to succeed. Relegation can mean loss of sponsorship, loss of advertising revenue and, above all, loss of good players. Some clubs striving for the top will do everything within their power and, if necessary, outside the regulations, to achieve their ambition, and once the goal posts are moved they are never returned to the same spot. In the present club system there is not enough money to sustain a professional game; nevertheless, the incentives being offered to players are putting an increasing strain on loyalty. Simon Geoghegan, the Irish winger, had signed registration forms for Wasps at the end of the 1994 season. He lived and worked in London, and had played at the club as a colt. Ye he chose instead to accept an invitation to play for Bath, with all the travelling and hassle that such a decision must entail. No one could blame him for wanting to play for the best club in the country in the company of so many good players, and in front of such big crowds. But in order to compete with Bath and their formidable drawing power, other clubs must be prepared to offer players an equally enticing environment.

The Rugby Football Union must therefore accept that the inevitable consequence of a league structure is another step towards professionalism. Nowadays clubs have to be more professional in their approach, hence the appointment of full-time salaried managers and directors of coaching. These people stand or fall by the results on the field, a business made all the more precarious by the fact that players have interests and demands on their time unconnected with rugby. In 1989 Wasps appointed Mark Taylor, the former All Black centre, as club coach. Taylor had played for Wasps in the early eighties and, along with luminaries like Roger Uttley, had had a profound influence in changing attitudes at the club. But he was an abrasive character with little sensitivity or understanding of the players' conflicting interests outside the game. This was especially true in London where there are so many competing demands on an individual's time. The very act of getting through the rush-hour traffic in time for training can present insurmountable difficulties, which Taylor could never accept. Because he had spent the whole day thinking rugby and planning for our success he expected the rest of us to be similarly fired and focused. Against personalities as phlegmatic but as strong as the likes of Paul Rendall, there were bound to be thunderous clashes, and a few weeks before we won the League Championship in 1990, Wasps and Taylor parted company. As club captain, who had naturally been very closely involved, I found it a particularly distressing affair, but it also demonstrated the dangers of living and working in the halfway house that rugby has now become.

Mention of Paul Rendall brings me to one of the game's most agreeable characters and one of the reasons why Sudbury was such a pleasant place to play rugby. A member of the old school whose pint and patter in the clubhouse after the game were as important to him as the game itself, he is, I fear, a dying breed. The younger players are spending far more time on the training field and far less in the bar afterwards. Rendall and Jeff Probyn were Tweedledum and Tweedledee. They were inseparable on the field, where they were bound together in that weird and wonderful freemasonry of the front row, and off it, where they would always share a room on tour, although how Rendall put up with Probyn's unsociable television-watching till three or four in the morning remains a complete mystery. Their best years coincided with Wasps' finest achievements between 1986 and 1990, when the club played in two cup finals, losing both to Bath, and won the League Championship. The 1987 final was close and furiously contested almost to the last, when Probyn was alleged to have collapsed a scrum, and Bath kicked the penalty. Probyn, always the picture of injured innocence on such occasions, was outraged by Fred Howard's decision, but with Simon Halliday scoring a try later in the game, his indiscretion probably wouldn't have mattered anyway.

Our league title was won almost by default but was nonetheless welcome and well deserved. It was just reward for the dedicated service and unswerving loyalty of club servants like Colin Pinnegar, David Pegler, Alan Simmons, Mark Rigby and Rob Lozowski. We had lost a couple of games earlier in the season but, as we always did in league competition, kept going doggedly to the last Saturday, when we were playing Saracens at home. Gloucester, the leaders, were at Nottingham, requiring only a point to win the title. A replica of the trophy had been despatched to Sudbury as a precaution, but nobody seriously expected Gloucester to lose. Our sole aim was to go out and enjoy ourselves against Saracens. With a couple of minutes of the match remaining and with Wasps holding an unassailable lead, word was passed on to the field that Gloucester had lost. The Championship was ours, and the celebrations continued far into the night. So far in fact that Steve Bates and I, who were due to join up with the England squad at the Petersham Hotel, didn't arrive until after midnight, very much the worse for wear. It wasn't until he got himself together the next morning that Bates discovered he had left his training kit back at the club. Wasps were often accused of being underachievers, an unfair charge against a club who were only once out of the top three in the first six years of the leagues' existence. Up to the end of the 1994 season Wasps had the distinction of being the only side to beat Bath in a league match at the Recreation Ground. This was courtesy of a last minute try following the unlikely mid-field combination of Mark Rigby and Fran Clough. But it is becoming harder to compete on level terms with clubs who have better resources and superior facilities.

I often wonder if the RFU fully realise the nature of the beast they have created. The power lies increasingly with the clubs, whose confidence and willingness to use it is growing. This was evident from the senior clubs' reaction to the television deal struck during the 1994 season between the RFU and Sky from which the RFU received £6 million. But the clubs, who were required to provide live action every week, were never consulted. They reacted furiously, naturally fearing a reduction in their support and gate receipts, and as a result a percentage of the television revenue was channelled their way. It was a small amount in comparison to the influence that the clubs now have on the English game, and the day cannot be far off when they will be prepared to fully exercise that power. There is another problem which has to be addressed. It concerns the intolerable burden being placed on the country's top players as administrators attempt to juggle the demands of the club, divisional and national commitments. Something has to give. Throught the 1993–94 season, and including England's tour to South Africa, a member of the national squad could have played as many as forty games. From the second week in September to the second week in June there were just three Saturdays free from competitive rugby. The conflict between club and country will reach its height in a World Cup year in which the competition is held in the southern hemisphere, when national interests would be best served by resting the squad from the end of the Five Nations Championship in March until the beginning of the tournament in May. But imagine the outcry from the clubs who are chasing championships and cups, or who are fighting to avoid relegation.

I am not at all sure that some of those responsible for running the game in England are fully aware of what is happening. The pace of change both at home and overseas is far outstripping their ability to adapt to it. But as a result of the vision and determination of a few, the pyramid so vital for England's survival at international level is now in place. It has taken nearly ten years to build. The problem now is to get the best players to the top. The system is there, the quality is not. Apart from those players who were injured and therefore not considered, the thirty players taken by England to South Africa in 1994 were generally deemed to be the best available. Compare that with the side which toured South Africa ten years earlier when there were none of the selectorial aids, such as the leagues and the divisions, by which to judge players. Even so, the 1994 side lost five out of their eight games in a country which had only recently returned to the international fold after many years of isolation and was still grappling with contemporary theory and modern practice. The fact that we shared the test series should not blind us to South Africa's production of high-quality players at a rate we cannot begin to match. They are spoilt for choice, which was one of their problems against England in the First Test, but if their selection process is still lodged in the dark ages, they do at least have the players. They also possess the structure, based as it always has been on their provincial rugby. It is the same in Australia and New Zealand. In England things are different. Historically the strength of our game has lain in the clubs and the counties, and with the diminishing status of the County Championship, the responsibility for quality production now rests exclusively with the clubs. The provincial system which underpins the game in South Africa, New Zealand and Australia would not work in England. There is in fact very little difference between Natal, Queensland and Auckland, and Bath, Leicester and Wasps, in that provincial sides in the southern hemisphere are basically club sides who train four times a week and play in a high-quality domestic championship. If there is a distinction to be made it is that provincial sides in South Africa, New Zealand and Australia openly admit to being semi-professional. There are, as we all know but many obstinately refuse to accept, a growing number of fully professional players stalking the rugby world. But now there is an even more ominous development which threatens to lift the provinces in the southern hemisphere to new heights. It is the Super Ten competition.

One of the biggest difficulties over the years has been the isolation of the southern hemisphere countries. Their domestic game has been played in a vacuum which has led to introversion. For so long they have cast envious eyes towards the Five Nations Championship and prayed for the day when they would have a similar competition circulating new ideas and introducing fresh talent. With the Super Ten, they have it. The competition enables the best players to perform in an élite structure, playing at a consistently higher pitch than their counterparts in England. It is quality, not quantity, that matters. The Courage Leagues have transformed the domestic game in England but, at the top level, there are too many matches and too few hard ones. With the greatest respect to some of the First Division sides, there are only four or five clubs capable of winning the Championship. The rest are simply not up to it, nor will they ever be until there is a radical change in thinking, particularly in the large cities. It is a dreadful indictment of the system that the three major centres outside London – Birmingham, Manchester and Leeds – between them have only one First Division club going into the 1994–95 season, and that club, Sale, represents a suburb of Manchester. Petty parochialism has been stifling our game for too long. The strength of northern rugby lies in Lancashire and Yorkshire, so why not two major clubs, one based in Manchester, the other in Leeds and both capable of competing with the best in England? If Newcastle/Gosforth, West Hartlepool and a few of the other neighbouring clubs were to unite in common purpose, Newcastle could also have a side worthy of the natural talent produced in that area.

Having been a staunch supporter of the Divisional Championship I am now convinced that it has outlived its usefulness, certainly in its present format. The clubs hold the key to the future of our game, but the structure must be streamlined to keep up with the changes taking place in the rest of the world. It is too much to expect our top players to turn out for eighteen league matches, plus cup and divisional games, on top of their commitments to the national side. What we need now is a competition similar to the Super Ten. The latter is one of the reasons why the South Africans, despite their prolonged exile and their naivety in certain aspects of the modern game, are catching up fast, and it is important that we react to it. So why not a European equivalent involving sides from England, Scotland, Wales, Ireland, France and Italy? Television companies would be falling over themselves to cover it, sponsors and advertisers would be lining up to be involved. Qualification for the competition could be: the top three sides in England (including the national cup holders); the top two sides in Wales (including the national cup holders); the club championship finalists in France; the club champions in Italy; the Irish inter-provincial champions; the Scottish inter-district champions.

There would be two pools of five, with each club playing the other clubs in the pool only once. The pool winners would meet in the final. An example might be:

Pool 1	Pool 2
Bath	Glasgow
Cardiff	Leicester
Montferrand	Swansea
Treviso	Toulouse
Ulster	Wasps

The competition would be run over five weeks, starting at the beginning of September and finishing in mid October. If the First Division of the Courage League was reduced to eight clubs playing home and away, league fixtures would then commence in mid October and run for fourteen Saturdays through to the end of the season. This would mean that the maximum number of competitive club games a player could play in a season, including Super Ten, league and cup, would be twenty-four. In a World Cup year there would obviously have to be special arrangements made, as there would to accommodate incoming touring sides, but I believe that a Super Ten series as I have outlined would have massive public appeal and would help us keep in step with developments overseas.

Having travelled the rugby world extensively, touring Australia, South Africa and New Zealand since 1991, I believe it would be fatal for us to be trapped by complacency. It took five years of blood, sweat and tears of frustration for England to reach the point where, in the space of nine months, they beat the All Blacks at Twickenham and the Springboks in Pretoria. Now we discover that the southern hemisphere countries are on the move again to an even higher plane. Seven years ago, when England were ignominiously knocked out of the World Cup, there was a forty-point gap between the countries in the two hemispheres, and believe me, that gap can very quickly open up again. Sharing a series against the Springboks doesn't change a thing. It merely demonstrates that England are fortunate in having a group of players, most of them products of a successful but increasingly antiquated system, who are good enough to hang on in against the best in the world. But unless we work to ensure that the next generation of players is given the chance to compete on level terms, then all the work of the last five or six years will have gone to waste. The only way we are going to achieve that is by broadening our horizons at home.

In the autumn of my career I cannot believe the changes that have taken place in the game over the last ten years. It is understandable that many of rugby's administrators who grew up with an entirely different game want to cling on to the values they hold dear and consider to be important. But it cannot be done. Personally, I would be very sad to see the game go fully professional and I would never want to be paid for playing. I cannot think of one player during my career who has, but there is a new breed of player coming into the game with a very different attitude. Whether or not it is good for rugby is another matter, but we cannot, must not, close our minds to the fact that the pace of change is accelerating all the time. It is a game which bears little resemblance to the one I first started playing at Barnard Castle School more than twenty years ago.

CHAPTER 8

Bladders, Blades and Blues

'Pale and haggard faces, lank and bony figures, children with the countenances of old men ... what an incipient Hell was breeding here.' The words, written by Dickens in *Nicholas Nickleby*, seemed particularly apt for the eleven-year-olds slogging over remote and rustic Durham terrain, in the intense cold of winter, clad only in vests, shorts and plimsolls. The grim apparition of Dotheboys Hall lay just up the road and although there was no one remotely resembling the villainous Wackford Squeers at Barnard Castle, it was a spartan existence for the boys. But it was one I grew to enjoy the longer I remained at the school. Never at any stage did I achieve academic brilliance, yet my attainments would have been very much worse had I not received such a solid grounding. Discipline was strict and we were made to work hard but that had never been a problem for me. I had been introduced to the work ethic at an early age by my parents Raymond and Mary who laboured seven days a week, fifty-two weeks a year on our dairy farm. Without the luxury of hired help, we all had to muck in, my two brothers, Richard and David, my sister Jayne and I. Even during the holidays from school and university there was work to do. I remember one Christmas, on the day before the Barbarians played Leicester, I was calving cows until the early hours of the morning. By the time we had finished there was no point in going to bed. I got into the car, drove to Welford Road and played, none too well probably, for the Baabaas.

Barnard Castle had an excellent academic reputation. It was also nationally renowned in the realms of sport for squash and swimming. As I have already recorded, swimming was not something at which I excelled and, despite the fact that after my near drowning in the first week of school I had learned to stay afloat, my style was closer to a doggy paddle than a recognisable stroke. It was, therefore, with some astonishment but immense pride that I was told of my selection for the class swimming team. This was my first big break in sport. I spent the morning switching between uncontainable excitement and high anxiety, but when I got to the swimming pool, kitted out and ready for the off, I discovered that the whole thing had been a rotten wheeze. In other sports, however, I began to show some promise. I never shared the dread and apprehension of some of the boys on those five-mile cross-country runs in the harshness of winter. I enjoyed diving into frozen puddles during rugby practice. At least I wouldn't drown in them. And above all I looked forward to the cricket season.

Cricket was my forte and we were extremely lucky in having the most enlightened of coaches in Kenneth King. He would spend hours after school throwing balls to us in the nets. Off drives, on drives, cover drives, forward defence, backward defence, for as long as we wanted to practise, Kenneth King stayed to help us. He was the archetypal Mr Chips. Barnard Castle was his life, having been a pupil at the school and having returned there to teach after his graduation from university. There have been countless classic techniques on the cricket fields of England and beyond which have owed everything to Kenneth King. A restless spirit, I wasn't content with batting. At school I also bowled medium pace, which meant that I was always in the action, either batting high up the order or opening the bowling.

It was the same in rugby. I chose fly half because of the constant involvement in the play. How Rory has stuck it out on the wing for all those years I'll never know. Unlike squash and swimming, the school had no great rugby tradition and, at that stage in my career, I had no great interest in it. I played most of the rugby season looking forward to the cricket term. Then John Oates arrived. He had come from Loughborough and had played for England Colts, but his rugby career had been shortened by a serious back injury. Both he and Nick Willings, the coach at Durham School who were our archrivals, were to have a major influence on my future in the game. Oates moulded a very fine 1st XV, one which was capable of competing with, and very often beating, the powerful Durham side. With Rory performing prodigious feats of try scoring – forty-one in fifteen matches – we played some wonderfully open rugby. Representative honours at school came in the minor and very brief form of Durham Schools, for whom I played against Yorkshire. We were thrashed and I was dropped. Along with Rory, I also joined the Middlesbrough Club, playing both cricket and rugby for them. My first appearance in the 1st XV was when I was still at school as a seventeen-year-old. I hadn't been able to get to training the week before the match, and found it a little daunting walking into the dressing room. The Middlesbrough front five were old stagers with years of experience. All of them had played for Yorkshire, and were totally underwhelmed at seeing me, thinking that I was the ball boy.

Everything that I have so far achieved in my life has come through hard work. It would be most satisfying to ascribe any success I have had to natural talent but it wouldn't be true. This has been as much the case in my studies as in my sport. In my year at Barnard Castle there were eight Oxbridge entrants. The standards were high and I had to work flat out to keep up. With my farming background I had decided to do my degree in Land Management, concentrating on the agricultural side rather than urban work. I had the academic qualifications to gain acceptance to Reading and Cambridge, where the Land Economy faculty was seen by many as the easy option. This was because it was a two-year course and tended to attract a number of talented postgraduate sportsmen. In defence of this vocational degree, a very high proportion of Land Economists have remained in the surveying profession. I wanted nothing more than to go to Cambridge. In the summer of my final exams at school I had gone up with a close friend, Richard Kent, to have a look round the colleges. Kent had been my scrum half partner in the 1st XV and we had opened the batting together. His uncle was a professor at one of the Cambridge colleges. Entering the city was like stepping into a different world. I was completely entranced by it and long before I had seen the magnificence of King's College Chapel, I knew that nothing else would suffice. But first I had to get through my interview. Ian Robertson tells the lovely story of how, at his admissions interview, the professor, a sports freak, tossed him a rugby ball. Not only did Robertson catch it but he then clinched his university place by drop kicking the ball into the waste-paper basket. The admissions tutor at St John's College, where I was hopefully bound, was Dr Peter Linehan whose sporting interest I had discovered was cricket. I played that card for all it was worth but whether it made a whit of difference I don't know. What I do know is that I must have been the last through the door before they shut it.

91

Going to Cambridge had a profound influence on my career, not so much in business but unquestionably in changing the course of my sporting life. Had I been refused entry to St John's I would have gone to Reading, whose reputation in Land Management was well established. Indeed it was probably held in higher esteem than the equivalent course at Cambridge. My professional life would therefore have been very similar to the one I am now pursuing. I would in all probability have ended up in London as a chartered surveyor operating in the urban sector. It is inconceivable, however, that my rugby career at Reading would have taken off as it did at Cambridge. Reading would have provided me with thoroughly enjoyable social rugby, which, at that time, was about the limit of my ambitions. But it could never have launched me into the international arena in the way that Cambridge did. What I was not prepared for was the speed with which events overtook me. For that I have to thank Nick Willings. In the few months between my final exams at Barnard Castle and going up to Cambridge, Willings had invited me to coach squash at Durham School. It was while I was there that I met John Kingston, the Cambridge captain, an old boy of Durham, who had returned to present colours to the school XV. Willings gave me a glowing reference and Kingston mentioned the possibility of my going up to Cambridge for pre-season training. It was only an aside so I thought no more about it. But not long afterwards I received a letter from Kingston inviting me to the training. I could hardly believe it. My track record as a schoolboy could not bear comparison with some of the distinguished undergraduates and postgraduates who were in attendance, players like Simon Smith and Mark Bailey, whose reputations in student rugby had already been established.

Bailey was the number one star, but I remember sitting in the stand watching the university play their traditional pre-season friendly against Cambridge City. Simon Smith was at his most majestic, scything through the opposition time and again with that perfectly balanced action of his. 'Christ,' I said to my companion next to me, 'what a superb player Smith is. A bloody sight better than that bloke Bailey.' Unfortunately for me, Bailey was sitting right in front of me and had heard every word. Generally, however, the gods – and Bailey, believe me, was one of them – have been extremely kind to me. I am a great believer in Fate. Nothing else could explain the extraordinary circumstances in which I found myself at the Sunderland rugby ground in that September of 1982, playing for the Dolphins against Cambridge University. After the pre-season training the university side went on a short tour to the north-east for which I was surplus to requirements. I therefore went home to the farm, but by way of a break decided to go over to watch the university play the Dolphins, an invitational side, at Sunderland. As luck would have it the Dolphins were short of a fly half and I was dragooned into playing. It was one of those games where everything I tried came off, including two drop goals from over forty yards.

That game was enough to win me a place on the Cambridge bench for the match against the Fijian tourists. At this stage Nick Chesworth, a former England schoolboy international and a post-graduate from Durham University, was the occupant at number ten and remained so for the early part of the season when the side were going well. But then they hit a rocky patch and, primarily because of my defence and my goal kicking, I was given my chance. I scored thirteen points in my first game, against Richmond, and twenty-one points against Northampton in my second. The most accurate barometer of the strength of the Cambridge back line was Ian Robertson. If it was above average then he would regularly stop off at Grange Road on his way to inspect his string of racehorses at Newmarket, in order to give us the dubious benefit of his coaching experience. When he never came near the place we knew we were in trouble. But in 1982 the backs were of sufficiently high calibre to attract his interest. In addition to Smith and Bailey, Robin Boyd-Moss, who went on to gain distinction as a cricketer, was in the centre along with Tim O'Brien, and John Cullen was at scrum half.

The training at Cambridge was the hardest I have ever encountered. It had to be if the students were to have any chance of survival against mature club sides like Gloucester, Leicester and Northampton. Our endurance work was supervised by Mike Turner, an athlete of considerable repute who was assistant manager of the Great Britain Olympic squad in Seoul in 1988. A 'Doc Turner', as it was nicknamed, consisted of thirty minutes' nonstop running at a variety of speeds from jogging to sprinting, at the end of which we were scarcely able to move. Even so, it was not enough to protect us when we came up against Gloucester later that season. With a pack containing Preedy, Mills, Blakeway, Fidler, Boyle and Teague, they pushed our scrum all over the field and inflicted terrible damage both physically and mentally. In the weeks before the Varsity Match there is an all-consuming fear of injury or illness. For most of the players it was an occasion which would never again be repeated in their rugby careers. It was the day towards which they had worked for months. They had talked about nothing else, they had thought about nothing else, and they lived for nothing else.

In 1982 Cambridge were the favourites. Their backs were strong, their forwards, led by John Kingston, were competent and well organised. For that, credit must go to Tony Rodgers who, we imagined, had been the Cambridge coach since the establishment of the university. As an ex-second-row forward he has what must be the unique distinction of producing a host of backs, but only a handful of forwards, who went on to win international recognition. Invariably late for training, the sight of Rodgers pedalling his bike towards Grange Road, his scarf and cauliflower ears flapping in the wind, will remain an imperishable memory of those halcyon days. The joy of university life lay in the extraordinary diversity of its talent. There were sportsmen and scholars, aesthetes and athletes, of different ages and from widely differing backgrounds. Rank, position, wealth seemed not to matter although, inevitably, there was an element of intellectual snobbery. But seldom did I move in such rarefied circles. Our social life centred more prosaically but less pretentiously on The Mill pub, where I was a more familiar figure than next door in the Land Economy library. As the baby of the Blues XV, I was taken under the wing of the final-year students, enjoying the best of both worlds with the university side and with my college set.

A mid-term crisis. We began losing heavily and I wondered whether this incredible journey which the Fates had set rolling at Sunderland was about to come to a crashing halt in the blood and grime of Gloucester. If there were to be changes, Kingston would have to make them at least three weeks before the Big Day. Please God, just one more chance, just one more week. The university team list was always pinned up in Ryder and Amies, the outfitters in King's Parade. Three weeks to go and I raced down to the shop, head and heart pounding, and there it was – number ten . . . C. R. Andrew. The following week I went even faster and was more of a flutter but the name, mercifully, was the same. Now all I had to do was to stay out of trouble. Ten days to go and Kingston, as tradition demands, went round the colleges taking the good news to the fortunate fifteen. I was in my little bedsit making fruitless attempts to concentrate on work when there was a knock at the door. It was Kingston. A blue in my first year, when the very height of my ambition had been a place in the college side, brought an indescribable feeling of pleasure and one which can never be repeated. The next few days passed in a bewildering kaleidoscope of photographs, kitting out, nervous anticipation, clamour, and the obligatory cocktail parties, the best of which was on the Sunday before the game, hosted by the club president at the home of Dr John Dingle. The toast was to the Club, the tipple was port and, glasses drained, we threw them into the fireplace chanting in unison, 'God damn bloody Oxford!'

Over the years the Petersham Hotel in Richmond has become like a second home to me. It has been England's base for Twickenham matches and traditionally it is where Cambridge teams stay before the Varsity Match. Whenever I start to take for granted my privileged position as an international sportsman, I think back to that occasion. The thrill and the glamour of it are unrepeatable but unforgettable. The police escort to the ground, the vast changing room, the peg with the light blue and white jersey bearing the number ten that I would be wearing. I was in a trance. Coming out of the dressing room last but one and hearing the roar of the crowd, I very nearly froze. My opposite number that day was one S. Barnes (St Edmund Hall) who had played in the match the previous year and who had acquired a reputation as a player of great promise. He had already become established at Newport having played representatively at schoolboy level for Wales and at under-23 level for England, with whom he had decided to throw in his lot.

The game ran more kindly for me than it did for Barnes. Even my first penalty kick at Twickenham was in the ideal position for a right-footed kicker – on the twenty-two, fifteen yards in from the left-hand touch-line. I scored twelve points in the match and Cambridge won 20-13. I played in two more Varsity Matches, in 1983 and 1984, both times on the winning side, but nothing came close to re-creating the wide-eyed wonderment of that day. There is nothing quite like the finality of defeat in a Varsity Match. With club, county or national sides there is always the opportunity the following week or during the next month to redress the balance, but not so in contests between Oxford and Cambridge. The winner takes all.

The loser, if he's extremely lucky, might get a second chance the following year, but for most the opportunity never repeats itself. For me, however, and for my parents who had come to watch the match, it was the start of a great adventure.

With the break-up of the 1982 Blues side after that match, I could turn my attention to work. If I was well ahead of schedule in sportsmanship I was far behind in scholarship. And if, as I hoped, the cricket season was to bear further fruit, I needed now to make up for time lost in my studies. Rugby was a minor diversion in terms of time compared to the all-consuming nature of cricket. Six days a week, very often seven, from April until the Varsity Match at Lords in mid July. Looking at the composition of the 1st XI that season, I realised that there would be little hope for a freshman to break into the established order. The captain was Stephen Henderson (Worcestershire and Glamorgan) and with him in the side were class players like Robin Boyd-Moss (Northamptonshire) and Tim Curtis (Worcestershire) who was later to play for England. Despite the fact that Henderson was at Magdalene College with John Kingston, the rugby captain, and that my good fortune had, up to now, known no bounds, I was resigned to sitting this one out and contenting myself with a few outings in the second team. In any case I had, to my surprise, been selected for the England Under-23 tour to Romania in May for which I required special dispensation from the eternally patient Peter Linehan. We came to a satisfactory accommodation. If I sacrificed cricket for work then I could go to Romania. It was Hobson's Choice, but by agreeing not to play cricket in that summer term, I had effectively chosen rugby ahead of what I had always considered to be my first love. In the space of a few short months my sporting priorities had been reversed. In fact I did manage to sneak in one or two games of cricket after the Romanian tour and was invited to go to Lord's for the Varsity Match as twelfth man. I even got on to the field as a substitute. Twickenham and Lord's in six months, and still only twenty.

The varsity cricket match is very different from its rugby equivalent. To begin with, the cricket match is played in the middle of the summer vacation when the students are down from the universities. The support tends therefore to be restricted to family and close friends. Nor is the build-up to the cricket match anything like as intense. It is one thing to focus all one's attention on an event lasting eighty minutes and something entirely different preparing for a contest spanning three days. For the cricketers who kept playing throughout the summer and who were to all intents and purposes like professionals in the amount of time they devoted to their sport, it was just another game. There was the excitement of playing against Oxford at Lord's, of course, but none of the passion, the pace and the pandemonium of Twickenham.

My second year at Cambridge was not appreciably different from my first. I moved from the Geography department into Land Economy, where my face was no more familiar to the lecturers and the library staff, and my attendances were every bit as infrequent. I played in another winning Cambridge side at Twickenham, the margin of victory on this occasion 20-9, my contribution once again twelve points, and, yet again, I went down on my knees to the saintly Dr Linehan. This time it was an Under-23 tour to Spain.

The cricket stars from the previous year had departed, leaving Cambridge with one of the most inexperienced sides for years. To make matters worse the captain, Angus Pollock, had been instructed by his professor not to play before his finals in May. We therefore had to manage without him for the early part of the season. So desperate was our plight that Ian Peck, a former captain of rugby and cricket who was now teaching at Bedford School, was invited to return as captain, bringing with him some much-needed experience and direction. The county sides enjoyed coming to Fenners. There was no pressure and, that year at least, precious little opposition. Their batsmen could get all the practice they wanted before the championship season began. Some of them, like Graham Gooch, took every opportunity to stay at the crease for as long as their stamina and daylight lasted. My recollection of those matches is fielding on the first day for five and a half hours and then, as an opening batsman, having to survive the last half-hour in the gathering gloom of a freezing April evening, very often against some hostile and deadly accurate bowling. The object was merely to block and stay until the next morning but, more often than not, a long and tiring day ended with a snick to first slip which meant an even longer and more tedious second day spent drinking endless cups of coffee and reading a few more chapters on inner-city development. It had become the tradition that the county sides batted first, a tradition that was famously broken on the occasion when Cambridge played

Leicestershire and Mike Atherton and David Gower, the respective captains, went out to the middle to toss up. 'There's not much point in tossing, is there?' said Gower. 'Whatever happens we'll bat first.' 'Not bloody likely,' was Atherton's response. 'If I win the toss we bat and you field.' Atherton always was his own man.

The evenings spent with the opposition in the pub after the match were always the best part of the day's cricket. A combination of Tetleys and tandoori turned Mike Gatting into one of the most environmentally unfriendly zones in England, but he was tremendous company, as were so many of the other professionals. On these occasions we would talk cricket long into the night. I knew that I would be more profitably employed back at St John's studying for the days, now terrifyingly close, when I would have to sit my exams, but to hell with it. This was the university of life I was attending. It was all part of my education.

This was not, however, a philosophy which won the wholehearted endorsement of my tutor. A first-class degree was now out of the question but who, other than nuclear scientists and college professors, needs a first-class degree? My view is that university should be about more than academic achievement. The camaraderie, the fellowship in sport, the time spent in the company of so many fascinating characters, the triumph in adversity, the acceptance of defeat, must be of greater practical value in the world outside than the cocooned narrowness of academia. There are few more infallible ways of judging a man than by playing sport with or against him, whether it be rugby, cricket or rowing. These are the three sports through which the universities of Oxford and Cambridge have gained worldwide fame and promotional exposure. For as long as time itself both seats of learning will be regarded first and foremost as places of academic distinction. That is as it should be. Academic values must never be compromised by the need to attract top-quality sportsmen. But in recent times there has been such an importance placed on scholarship over sportsmanship that it has, in my opinion, been to the detriment of university life.

It has undoubtedly had a melancholy effect on the standards of rugby and cricket at both universities. Yet both have retained their privileged positions in first-class competition, the rugby sides continuing to play many of England's top clubs and cricket holding on to its fixtures against the counties. In the two years of my involvement in cricket at Cambridge I played for the Combined Universities against Clive Lloyd's West Indians and Allan Border's Australians. It was an honour to do so but it seemed to me to be carrying privilege and tradition too far for two universities playing to a level not much above school standard to be given fixtures against the best teams in the world game. The establishment of league rugby has inevitably meant a loss of status for the universities, if not in the fixture list then certainly in the quality of opposition put out by the clubs, who seldom field their first teams. The leagues have also meant that talented young players with university potential are being persuaded that their rugby ambitions are more likely to be met by remaining with their clubs than by taking a year or more out at university. Some clubs are pulling out all the stops to foster that notion. Cricket is more fortunate in that the universities still have a part to play in the first-class game, if only as an early season punchbag for the counties. They also contribute to the Combined Universities side which plays in the Benson & Hedges competition, eligibility for which has now been extended beyond Oxford and Cambridge to embrace all the universities in Britain. But when one considers that some of the greatest names in cricketing history have been nurtured at Cambridge – May, Dexter, Brearley, Majid Khan, to name a few – it is sad to see the decline in standards and status. Unless the universities act quickly to reverse the trend in rugby and cricket as Cambridge has done very dramatically in rowing, then I fear for the future of both sports.

In 1984, Cambridge cricket was not up to much. Few gave us any chance against an Oxford side containing Andy Miller and John Carr of Middlesex, Kevin Hayes of Lancashire, and the aptly named Giles Toogood, who almost single-handedly won the Varsity Match that year. He scored 52 not out in the first innings and 109 in the second. My performance in that match was as disappointing as my form had been throughout the season. Quite how I was selected to play for the Combined Universities against the West Indies I will never know. Desmond Haynes and Gordon Greenidge opened the batting. Viv Richards, Larry Gomes and Clive Lloyd followed them, and when they had finished smashing us to all parts of the ground, Joel Garner and Eldine Baptiste put the frighteners on our batsmen. I like to think that it was my subtle variation of offspin and flight which deceived Haynes but, on reflection, I think it more likely that between the ball leaving my hand and reaching his bat, he had gone to sleep.

Whatever the reason, I got him out. On the debit side I had come in to bat at number five, and had purred with satisfaction at seeing off both quickies only to fall to the gentle spin of Richards. Remarkably, we drew the match. The following year the game against the touring Australians was at Fenners, and as captain of Cambridge I was asked to lead the combined side. It was my first summer at the university without rugby. I had been selected for England's tour to New Zealand but had to withdraw because of my final examinations. It had given me the chance to spend a little time sharpening my batting and I had put together some impressive scores. My maiden first-class century had come against Nottinghamshire at Trent Bridge three weeks before the match against Oxford, and I had made 84 against Essex in the Benson & Hedges competition. It was in that match that Graham Gooch hit the hardest cover drive I have ever seen. I was pretty reasonable in the field and was normally posted at cover, but on this occasion the ball flashed past me and had hit the advertising boards on the boundary before I had even moved.

We had some richly entertaining characters in the Cambridge side that year. Charlie Ellison, the brother of Richard who played for England, and Archie Cotterell from Downside were relics of a bygone age. Both were true Corinthians. They were naturally talented sportsmen but showed scant respect for the modern sporting conventions of psychological and physical preparation. Their idea of fitness training was sprinting to the pub before closing time. We even tried to shame them into at least looking fit by supplying them with tracksuits, but to no avail. Charlie, bleary-eyed and tousled, would often come cycling into Fenners long after play had started. But in a sport in which so many hours are spent in each other's company and where time can hang so heavily, characters like Ellison and Cotterell were indispensable. There was another gifted but temperamental sibling in our side, Paul Roebuck, whose brother Peter is acquiring as much of a reputation as a writer on the game as he did as a player. It was on Roebuck that our last slender hopes of saving the Varsity Match rested in 1985. It marked my farewell to the university and to student life. I wanted so much for it to be a triumphant departure and, after my failure with bat and ball in the previous year's match, I was hoping to leave in style. But we had done little right on the first two days. I had scored 12 in each innings and Cambridge were on the brink of defeat. Only Roebuck and Tony Lea of the recognised batsmen remained, when play started on the third day and all hope seemed to have gone. I wanted to be alone with my thoughts, so I climbed to the upstairs balcony at Lord's for a few moments of quiet contemplation. On the way up I caught a snatch of a radio report about bad weather interrupting play at Wimbledon. But the clouds were too high in St John's Wood for any likelihood of rain. I sat down and began to reflect on the three happiest years of my life. I had run out on to the Twickenham turf, I had walked through the Long Room and on to the wicket at Lord's. I had played in the company of some of the world's greatest practitioners of rugby and cricket and I had somehow scraped a decent degree. Such a pity that it was going to end in the disappointment of defeat. And then, from heaven, via Wimbledon, came that big, black, beautiful cloud. Play abandoned, match drawn and, once again, Fate had come to my rescue.

CHAPTER 9

Far Pavilions

If ever there was a time when the choice between rugby and cricket hung in the balance, then it was during that summer of 1985 after I left Cambridge. Without the distraction of rugby I had been able to concentrate on the sport which continued to occupy a special place in my affections and at which I still considered myself to be more proficient. My cricket had improved quite dramatically in my final term at Cambridge, despite the personal disappointment of a poor showing in the Varsity Match. The century against Nottinghamshire had attracted the interest of the club's cricket manager, who had approached me about the possibility of joining the playing staff at Trent Bridge. I was going to start my first job in surveying with a firm in Nottingham in September and my digs was conveniently situated next door to the ground. But I was a Yorkshireman born and bred and if I was going to play county cricket anywhere, it would be at Headingley. Earlier that season Cambridge had played the MCC, a side captained by Richard Hutton which had also included Geoff Boycott. Both were Yorkshiremen, both had captained England, and they had one other thing in common – an intense dislike of each other. They were from completely different backgrounds, equals in some ways but opposites who failed to attract, and not once during the course of that match did a word pass between the two.

Boycott was recovering from injury and was using the game to get his eye in. He was doing very well too until I beat him all ends up, tempting him into an uncharacteristically rash shot to mid-on. I may not have taken many wickets in first-class cricket but with Desmond Haynes and Geoff Boycott on my list of victims, no one can argue about the quality. In the bar afterwards, Boycott came over for a chat. He knew about my background and that I had been offered a short-term contract, very much on a trial basis, to play for Yorkshire seconds. We talked about style and technique and the problems of making the grade at first-class level. In many ways my style was similar to Boycott's. I had a good defence and a number of scoring shots without having a wide range of strokes. I was weak on the leg side, strong on the off and preferred to play off the front foot. Despite the fact that I had scored a half-century against the MCC, Boycott had spotted a number of technical failings. The key, he said, was not to commit myself to the shot too early, otherwise there would be no time to readjust. Against that, if I left it too late before picking up the line and length and shaping to play the shot, then it would be impossible to get my feet into the right position. Graeme Hick is a good example of a front-foot player who occasionally gets his footwork horribly wrong. Boycott also made the point that whilst my technical flaws might escape punishment on the slow wicket at Fenners, they would be exposed on the faster tracks around the country.

I knew what he meant. A few weeks previously against Sussex I had been introduced to the real world of pace bowling. The bowler was the six-foot-eight-inch South African, Garth le Roux, whose short-pitched delivery I had the temerity to pull for four through mid-wicket. The next ball was also pitched short of a length but this time it came down five times faster. I was rooted to the spot, and my bat had scarcely moved from the crease when the ball smashed into my helmet, ripping out the bolt that secured the visor. There is, I suppose, an element of bravery required to stop a mighty second-row forward in full flight, but it takes a different sort of courage to withstand the sustained onslaught of fast bowling. The most pulverisingly accurate example of that was when Courtney Walsh eventually unhinged Mike Atherton in a spell of relentless savagery during the Second Test in 1994. Watching Walsh on his run-in to the wicket reminded me of the story of David Lloyd, the Lancashire and England opener, facing his first delivery from Malcolm Marshall. As Marshall made his way back almost to the sight screen to begin his run-up, Lloyd quailed, 'Bloody 'eck – I don't go as far as that on me 'olidays!' The most menacing bowler I ever faced was the West Indian, Patrick Patterson. Yorkshire seconds were playing their Lancashire equivalents on a dank day at Doncaster and, despite the presence of Atherton, Neil Fairbrother and Patterson in the opposition, Yorkshire were on top. Patterson in his frustration and fury began to work up to test match pace. Nothing in my experience had been quite so terrifying.

It was during my spell with Yorkshire that I began to appreciate the harshness of life as a professional cricketer. Even those few who make the grade at county level gain small financial reward. For every Ian Botham whose fame and fortune has been secured by cricket, there are countless club pros eking out a living on the county circuit in the summer who struggle even harder to make ends meet in the winter. I had been told by Phil Carrick that I might possibly have a future with the county side but that it would require a dedication and commitment to the sport which I doubted that I could give. I therefore took the decision, albeit reluctantly, to cut the cord and settle for the lower, more social orders of village cricket. I still wonder to this day whether I did the right thing. I derived more satisfaction and enjoyment out of batting well than from any other sporting activity, and like the relative of Lord Home who couldn't walk down the aisle of a church without wondering whether it would take spin, I can never shake myself free of cricket's influence.

There are many more unpleasant places to be on a Sunday afternoon in May than Thame cricket ground. But that afternoon in 1989 my mind was twelve thousand miles away, with the Lions in Australia. I had been bitterly disappointed at being left out of the touring party. I had played well in the Five Nations Championship, as well certainly as Craig Chalmers and Paul Dean, the fly halves who had been selected. My round of golf with the Lions' assistant coach, Roger Uttley, after the announcement of the side, had been more therapeutic than instructive. At least I had got things off my chest but, quite properly, he had told me little about the reasoning behind the decision not to take me. 'Hang on in there, keep yourself fit and you never know what might happen' was the most comfort I could extract from him. So I returned my attentions, somewhat peevishly, to cricket and was playing that Sunday afternoon for Gerrards Cross against Thame.

The Lions had played the opening match of their tour the previous day against Western Australia in Perth and I had been more than a little interested to hear a radio report that Dean had left the field with a knee injury. It was occupying my mind as we strolled in for the tea interval. There was a message for me. 'Someone called John Gasson wants you to phone him urgently.' Now, in all my years with

Wasps there has hardly ever been a time when John Gasson, the club's devoted and incredibly conscientious press officer, didn't want to engage me in urgent discussion. Furthermore, the tea interval lasted twenty minutes and I hadn't yet had a telephone conversation with John lasting less than half an hour. In all probability he was going to tell me the news I already knew – that Dean had been injured. But the answer to my problem lay in my pocket – ten pence was all the loose change I had, two minutes maximum, so I took the plunge. John's first words were all I needed to hear to set my pulse racing. 'Bob Weighill has been trying to contact you. Can you call him immediately.' That could mean only one thing. Paul Dean was out of the tour and the Lions were summoning me as his replacement. My old friend Fate had turned up trumps again, although, naturally, I felt deeply sorry for Dean. There had been rumours even before the Lions' departure that his knee was troubling him, and a more detailed examination, twenty-four hours after the Western Australia game, confirmed that he would be unable to take any further part in the tour.

Arrangements were made for me to fly out on the Tuesday, which gave me one day to make all the necessary preparations, including breaking the news to Debenham Tewson & Chinnocks that they would have to soldier on without me for the next six weeks. They assured me that they had been doing well enough without me for the last two years and were, as always, generously accommodating and genuinely delighted at my good fortune. As luck, or in this case, bad luck would have it, my appearance at the Lions' hotel in Brisbane coincided with the team's arrival from Melbourne where they had been playing the midweek match against Australia B. The first person I bumped into, quite literally, was poor Paul Dean on crutches. Words seem so utterly feeble on such occasions. The rest of the party, though, were in good spirits. Two wins in their first two games and victory against a highly charged Queensland side in the third game were a massive boost to morale. It also set the alarm bells ringing throughout Australia. Queensland, with their big, bruising pack, had come off second best in the physical battle. The squealing and whingeing from the Queensland camp after the match was music to our ears. The Lions were ahead in the psychological battle as well.

My tour was very nearly the shortest on record. Along with the other dirt-trackers I went out after the Queensland match for some sprint training. Craig Chalmers, who had come on as the replacement for Dean against Western Australia, had played three games in a row and, as the relief fly half, I would be expected to play in the next midweek match. My legs were still stiff from the journey, I overstretched and felt that numbing sensation at the back of my thigh. A hamstring pulled, tweaked or torn, I didn't know which but I stopped immediately and made straight for Kevin Murphy's treatment table. A wee treasure is Murphy. Not only is he an outstanding physiotherapist but he can be trusted to keep a secret. At least for as long as it can prudently be kept a secret. He would never put a player's physical well-being at risk nor would he jeopardise the chances of the team by hiding an injury from the management. But for now I needed his silence and, more importantly, his healing powers. By the time I ran out at Cairns against a Queensland Country XV wearing the Lions scarlet for the first time and heavily strapped around the thigh, Murphy had convinced me that I was a hundred per cent fit. I convinced myself of that fact after a forty-yard break which put Chris Oti over for a try. I even managed to take the goal kicks, and the Lions won again.

I often wonder what would have happened to the Lions and to their impressive record if they had lost a couple of games early in the tour. There lay within the touring party, selected heavily from England and Scotland, the seeds of its own destruction. With Ian McGeechan as coach and Finlay Calder as captain, there was a strong Scottish influence in team selection. Calder, along with John Jeffrey and Derek White, had formed the Scottish loose trio in the 1989 Championship. Mike Teague, Dean Richards and Andy Robinson were the English back-row forwards on the tour and there was, at times, undisguised rivalry between the two sets. The feeling among the English contingent that Calder wasn't playing well enough to win a test place ahead of Robinson was obviously not shared by McGeechan, but after the Queensland game, in which Calder had come closer to his known form, selection of the pack for the First Test was made very much easier. Teague and Richards, the two outstanding players on the tour, were never under serious threat, although an injury subsequently forced Teague out of the test. Nor was Paul Ackford's place at lock in doubt, and the front row of Sole, Moore and the Welshman, Dai Young, had submitted an unanswerable case against Queensland. Bob Norster, more on the strength of his game against Wade Dooley in the Home Championship than for his tour form, was Ackford's second-row partner for the First Test in Sydney. There was less certainty about the composition of the backs. Injuries to Scott Hastings and John Devereux and a reluctance to gamble on the sublime but unpredictable skills of Jeremy Guscott contributed to the selectors' dilemma at centre, and eventually they settled on the solid virtues of Brendan Mullin and Mike Hall.

At no stage during the game did the Lions' midfield function satisfactorily, which was, more than anything else, due to the failure of the forwards to exert any measure of control at the set piece. The balance of the back row had been fatally disturbed by the injury to Teague, whose replacement, Derek White, never came to terms with the pace of the game. Given their forward superiority in the provincial games this was a mighty blow to the tourists and proved to be an insurmountable handicap. A terrible depression fell on the team at the end of the game. Australia had dismantled the Lions in every area, scoring four tries to none and winning by a record margin of 30-12. It was now that Clive Rowlands, the Lions manager, came into his own. He had the Welsh gift of the gab and this was the moment for one of his finest soliloquies. The dressing room at the Sydney Football Stadium is partitioned, with the team in one half and the replacements, other team members and general hangers-on in the other. Rowlands called us all together. Somehow he succeeded in lifting us from the depths of despair and he finished his speech by pointing to the Lions badge on his blazer. 'From this point on, lads,' he said, 'the badge is going to get bigger.' The team stayed together that night. We went off to a club in Darling Harbour and tried as best we could to drown our sorrows. But this was Australia, where there were constant reminders of our failure. The savage Lions had become puny pussy cats. The Australian media went to work on us as only they can. We were ridiculed, we were mocked and some of the press comments in the aftermath of the test bordered on the libellous. Without question some Australian supporters are the most ungracious and querulous in defeat, the most obnoxiously arrogant in victory.

We moved on to Canberra for the next game, against Australian Capital Territory, still in a state of shock. No one had been more profoundly affected by the test result than Ian McGeechan. He took the defeat personally and it required all Rowlands' skills as a motivator to get his coach back on course. After twenty minutes of the game in Canberra it looked as if the tour was heading for oblivion. The Lions were 18-4 down and a second humiliation now seemed inevitable. But our forwards dug deep into their reserves of strength and character. Gradually, with the backs providing some sweet moves, we began to turn the game round, eventually winning 42-25. It was one of the few occasions in my experience when the non-playing members of the side rushed from the stand to applaud the players as they came off the field. Everyone recognised the importance of the victory in repairing our damaged morale. It was also clear that changes would be made to the side for the Second Test at Brisbane on the Saturday. Scott Hastings and Jeremy Guscott, who had played effectively as a centre combination in Canberra, would be given the chance to operate together against Australia, and I was selected in place of Chalmers at fly half. The Scotsman had played impressively on tour and it was his drop goal in the last minute which had won the game against New South Wales the week before the First Test. But he still lacked experience, which was only to be expected of a player in his first season of international rugby. After five years at that level it was felt that I would bring stability to the side. Moreover, I was at last sustaining the consistency which my game had lacked in the past. At no point during the tour did the Lions look entirely convincing in the quality of their back play. This both perplexed and frustrated McGeechan, who wanted to develop the game beyond the boundaries of the forwards. One of the reasons for our difficulties lay in the forward strategy, which was an uneasy blend of English mauling and Scottish rucking. Basically, the idea was to ruck going forward and to maul going back but, as with so many compromises cobbled together, the best of both worlds lost out to the worst elements of the coalition.

The two other changes in the side for the Second Test were on the blindside, where Teague returned after injury, and at lock, where Wade Dooley replaced Norster. This shocked the Welsh contingent but something had to be done to combat the sheer size of the Australian locks, Steve Cutler and Bill Campbell, and at six feet eight inches, Dooley had the physical presence which Norster lacked. After team practice one day, Uttley had taken the forwards away for a heart-to-heart. A magnificent forward in his playing days and a sincere man, Uttley was not perhaps in the Henry V class as an orator, but clearly he had worked hard on this motivational lecture. He picked out one forward after another – 'David Sole, the most mobile prop in the world . . . Brian Moore, the most competitive hooker in the world . . . Paul Ackford, the best front jumper in the world . . . Mike Teague, the hardest tackler in the world . . . ' and so on until he came to Dooley. 'And Dooley – you're replacing Bob Norster, the best line-out jumper in the world, the best lock forward in the world – you're in the side because you're . . . BIG.'

There were some mighty big Lions performances in that Second Test at Ballymore. The tone was set at the very first scrummage, when Robert Jones stood on Nick Farr-Jones's foot. The Australian reacted angrily and the next moment the Jones boys were grappling on the ground in an unsightly tangle. The Welshman, with that classic pass off both hands and woundingly accurate box kick, also had a temper. I have never felt more comfortable more quickly with any other scrum half. We settled into each other's game from our very first serious practice together, which, because of my partnership with Gary Armstrong in the midweek side, had been just four days before the test. Jones and one or two others had been lathering up in the changing room before the match. Never have I seen more pent-up fury, more raw emotion, than there was before kickoff that day. If such naked desire to win could only be harnessed and bottled it would provide the formula for everlasting success. I experienced it before the 1993 Lions played the Second Test against New Zealand in Wellington, before England's game later that same year against the All Blacks at Twickenham and before England's First Test against South Africa at Loftus Versfeld in the summer of 1994. But never to quite the same pitch as it was at Ballymore in 1989. It was all too much for Dean Richards, a product of the silent and contemplative school of self-motivation, who walked out of the changing room. Each to his own. Richards produced yet another colossal performance on the field that day.

At the end of the series, Bob Dwyer, the Australian coach, wrote that the Lions were the dirtiest team he had ever seen on an international field and that out roughhouse tactics had been persistent and deliberate. That was utter nonsense. Throughout the tour, Australian sides had boasted about their physical supremacy. Before the New South Wales game we could even hear the banshee screeching of 'One in, all in' from the opposition dressing room. The simple truth is that the Lions were harder physically and mentally than the opposition, and the Australians couldn't take it. There was, admittedly, one unpardonable act of brutality in the Second Test from Dai Young, who was extremely lucky not to be sent off for stamping. But at no stage during the tour had the Lions gone out with a plan to intimidate the opposition. We had, of course, identified the danger men. Nick Farr-Jones was one, David Campese was another, and there can be no question that we got to Campese during the series.

The Lions had spent most of the Second Test trying to catch up. Going into the final quarter we still hadn't succeeded. Gavin Hastings had kicked a penalty and I had dropped a goal but we were 12-6 down. To make matters worse, Hastings had taken a knock on the head and was quite obviously in a different world from the rest of us. We were awarded a penalty on the right-hand side of the field, fifteen metres in from touch. Calder, recognising that he couldn't entrust Hastings with the kick, tossed the ball to me. 'Get on with it,' he said brusquely. To this day that kick is the most important I have ever taken. The margin was down to three points and the Lions were going into the home straight the stronger side. If the try which turned the game and the series was hardly a classic, it was nevertheless a major landmark in Lions history. A pass from Scott Hastings so bad that it bounced, Barnes Wallis-like, into his brother's arms defied conventional defence. The gap opened up and Gavin, who probably remembers nothing of it, scored. Minutes later, Robert Jones twice exposed Campese's fallibility under the high ball. The forwards drove and Guscott, with the elegance and arrogance which were to be his trademarks, audaciously grub-kicked through the Australian defence to score under the post.

In the bareness of the score line, 19-12, history will not record that the Lions had been much less dominant than they were in the deciding test the following week, when the margin of victory was a slender one point, 19-18. This match will forever be remembered as the occasion when a moment's loss of concentration by Campese cost Australia the game and the series. I had miscued an attempted drop kick so badly that Campese fielded the ball out on the wing. But instead of playing safe he made as if to open out and passed it to his full back, Greg Martin, who was stationed in his in-goal area. Caught unawares, Martin dropped the ball and Ieuan Evans pounced to score. When the final whistle blew, some of us did a lap of honour carrying a Union Jack. How the Aussies hated that! The purring pussy cats had turned back into roaring lions and by the time Clive Rowlands came down to join in the celebrations, the Lions badge, which had been getting bigger with every day since our defeat in the First Test, had outgrown the blazer.

We had come through a lot; the sniping and derision from the Australian press; the allegations of dirty play, fuelled by the hypocritical condemnation of the Lions by the Australian Rugby Union, who had had the effrontery to pass a series of resolutions on foul play prior to the Third Test; and the persistent taunts of the home supporters. We had silenced them all and no one in the party was more relieved and overjoyed than Finlay Calder. He had been the target of a good deal of criticism, much of it from the British press and most of it unwarranted. He had not played well in the early part of the tour and had Andy Robinson been fully fit, Calder might well have found himself under more pressure. But he had the character and the determination to come through his ordeal and had played outstandingly well in both winning tests. I had roomed with him in the week before the Third Test when the team had a short but welcome break at Surfer's Paradise. We had much in common. He was a quiet, shy man with a tendency to bottle things up, a characteristic which Sara is forever telling me that I have. Winning the test at Ballymore gave him a new lease of life. He was a different person from that point on.

Unusually, the final test did not mark the end of the tour. We had two more games to play, the first against a New South Wales Country XV who attempted the most bizarre move ever seen on a rugby field when their fly half ran over the backs of the forwards in the scrum, only to be flattened by Gary Armstrong as he came down the other side. The game was played at Newcastle, which purported to be a holiday resort offering hunting, fishing, shooting and women. I cannot, of course, speak with any authority on the last-named delight but if it was anything like the other pastimes on offer, it wouldn't have been up to much. A cricket match was organised, if that is the right word. It was, in fact, a shambles and never in my life have I seen so many hopelessly uncoordinated batting techniques. But the competitive spirit burned as brightly in the final over, when Peter Dods required one hit to win the match, as it did in the palpitating climax to the final test. Steve Smith from Ballymena, who had sampled every drop of Guinness in the country, got Dods out to complete his hat trick and win the match. The final game of the tour was against an Anzac XV. The side had been gravely weakened and the fixture grossly devalued by the refusal of so many top New Zealanders to play in the match. Only three turned up, Steve McDowell, Kieran Crowley and Frano Botica. It turned out to be a most entertaining and enjoyable game which the Lions won 19-15, a testament to the endurance and unquenchable spirit of the team, who by now had other things on their minds.

I certainly did. Six weeks later I was getting married to Sara. As usual, the arrangements had been left to her. It was one of the few weddings during our lives together at which we have both managed to be present. Almost invariably I have been away on rugby tours, with the result that I have missed the weddings of most of our friends, including the splicing of my best man, Andy Davies, with whom I had played cricket at Cambridge. Knowing my unreliability on such occasions, he had taken the precaution of organising two best men, which was just as well, because I was playing for Toulouse in the club championship quarter-final against Dax. There was a counter-attraction on our wedding day of 18 August. A World XV were on tour in South Africa as part of the South African Rugby Board's centenary celebrations. Approaches had been made to us in Australia when it was mooted that the Lions should participate in the celebrations. The invitation was discussed by the players and it was agreed that we would go as a team or not at all. We named our price, which was one the South Africans were not prepared to pay. Instead they began to court individual players who were, in turn, put under pressure by senior administrators in the game. While some members of the International Board were encouraging players to take part, others were warning that acceptance of the South African invitation would endanger their international careers. There is no limit, it seems, to the hypocrisy within the game's administration. During our wedding a phone call came through for Steve Bates, inviting him to go out. He refused, but those players who accepted the invitation to play were undoubtedly well remunerated for their efforts.

The affair had splintered the unity of the Lions party and was to have repercussions at the beginning of the next domestic season when a Lions XV was due to play France in Paris in yet another celebratory match, this time to mark the bicentenary of the Republic. Once again the Lions who had toured Australia agreed on presenting a united front to officialdom. We requested that all thirty players on the tour should be invited to attend the match, along with wives and girlfriends. The request was rejected out of hand by the Four Home Unions. Many of the players nobly stood by the original agreement and flatly refused to play in the game, but a number of us began to recognise that 'sticking to one's principles' can very often be a euphemism for bloody-minded obstinacy. Whatever we decided, the game was going to be played. Better, we thought, to have a sizeable representation of those who had done the Lions proud in Australia than a scratch side comprising players who had not been good enough to have been selected for the tour. In the event there were only two players, Damien Cronin and Dave Egerton, who had not been in Australia and, in an enthralling contest, the Lions, whom I was proud and privileged to captain, won 29-27.

The Lions tour of 1989 marked a turning point in my career. Up until then I had questioned my ability to stay with the world's best. At the top of my form I knew I could compete, but my problem had been one of inconsistency. Too often I fell below my best. The confidence and self-esteem I gained from that tour has remained with me through the good, the bad and the indifferent. For that I will always be grateful to the Lions. As a boy I was an avid reader of the Lions' exploits in New Zealand and South Africa. A Lions tour was for me, as it is for all players in Britain and Ireland, the ultimate goal. There is nothing like it, and that is as true for our players as it is for Australians, South Africans and New Zealanders, particularly the latter two countries, where the Lions traditions are so strong. Yet I believe that the Lions are living on borrowed time. The advent of the World Cup has given the game another dimension and has brought a new and perhaps higher goal into the sights of the players. If anyone doubts that, just ask a player the one simple question: 'You have a choice – to play for your country in the World Cup or to play for the Lions. Which is it to be?' The answer, I suspect, almost without exception, would be to play in the World Cup. In New Zealand in 1993 there were mutterings of discontent and disenchantment from some of the Lions for whom the tour had failed to come up to expectations. When the team is successful, as it was in 1989, the concept of the four countries united in a common cause works wonderfully, but too seldom has it been successful. One of the problems is that there is no life after the Lions. Once the tour is over the party is disbanded. The players go their separate ways, back to their own countries, and are unlikely ever again to come together as a team. If the Lions are to have a future I believe that serious consideration should be given to awarding them a home series against major touring sides. A three-match series against the All Blacks, the Springboks or the Wallabies would be a massive attraction and would help save the Lions from extinction. This would not have to be at the expense of the individual countries, who would continue playing international matches against the tourists. Are England, Scotland, Ireland and Wales any stronger opponents than Auckland, Transvaal and Queensland? Probably not. It would be a much harder, more demanding and, perhaps, longer itinerary for the tourists. But then we are in the age of the semi-professional – aren't we?

CHAPTER 10

For Love or Money?

Amateurism. Like scrum caps, leather studs and dubbin, it has long since disappeared from the game's landscape. A noble but unsustainable doctrine and, in an international context at least, now removed from the lexicon of rugby terminology. Rugby at international level is big business, and even at club level it is a middle-sized business. It requires a professional outlook and professional expertise to keep it afloat. Some older relics of Jurassic Park cling to the notion that amateurism still exists, but those of us who travel the world as international players know better. There is no longer a place for the amateur ethic, no matter how much we may mourn its passing and I confess to being one of the mourners. Amateurism has much to commend it and despite the inexorable shift towards a semi-professional game, it is what still distinguishes rugby union from other major sports. Rugby gets to the parts few other sports can reach. The self-employed carpenter packs down in the same scrum as the company lawyer, forging a mutual respect and an everlasting bond of friendship. The catalyst is amateurism. The uniqueness of the game is inextricably bound up in the richness of the characters who play it. They come from different backgrounds and have a wide range of different interests but they all share a love of rugby. Love is all, or nearly all, there is. There could be no other motives for playing the game and if we all lived by the same rules, then in all probability that is the way it would remain. But in this, as in so many other aspects of the game, the rugby world is unable to present a united front.

In the long term, the only way that England can keep up with South Africa, New Zealand and Australia is for our players to become semi-professional. Those of us who toured with England to

South Africa in 1994, and those administrators who accompanied us, were staggered by what we saw and heard. There is little doubt that some of the leading South African players are full-time professionals. They are paid retainers from their provinces and receive match fees of between £200 and £400 per match. There were also rumours of six-figure sums being paid to players who switched provinces. Their so-called jobs enable them to devote most of their time to the game. Provincial players train three or four afternoons a week and spend many more hours in individual practice. How can those of us in this country, holding down responsible jobs, possibly compete with that?

In a conversation with Steve Redgrave, the Olympic oarsman, I received an insight into the workload of a full-time international sportsman. He trains in one shape or form every day of the week. He permits himself between two and three weeks off every year, and the longest break he has ever taken was six weeks after the Barcelona Olympics. One day without training makes the work that little bit harder the next, so he rarely has a day off. We talk earnestly about commitment to rugby but we don't begin to compare, nor could we live, with the strictness of that regime.

To change the status of rugby from amateur to professional would be to alter the nature of the sport. The tunnel vision mentality of a Redgrave, a Faldo or a Sampras is still a million miles away from the world of an international rugby player in England who can manage, albeit with increasing difficulty, to fit his pastime around his family life and business affairs. He still enjoys the freedom of amateurism. He is not contractually bound by his club to appear on demand at a time and place of his employer's choosing. He can still go out in front of sixty thousand spectators and play the game on his terms without heed or concern for those who have paid good money to watch him. And the game is still recognisable as the one which was played thirty years ago. But for how long?

Consider how many sports have fallen prey to the paying public's insatiable desire to be entertained. Cricket, with its wall-to-wall scheduling of one-day matches, is one example. Rugby league, with its constant, if often monotonous, movement is another. And Wimbledon, the greatest tennis tournament in the world, is coming under threat. The dimensions of the court are the same as they were when Fred Perry was a boy, but no longer can they accommodate the size and strength of today's players or the speed at which they play the game. Smaller racket heads, bigger courts and the reduction to one serve have been put forward as ideas for increasing the entertainment level of a sport which, on grass at any rate, has become a predictable procession of serve and volley played in the main by a group of charmless robots. The recent law changes in rugby, hatched in Australia and New Zealand and aimed at speeding up the play and making it more spectator-friendly, have been forced through without any consideration as to how they might alter the character of the game. But this is the price that sport has to pay for selling its independence, and those in authority who warn of the consequences of a shift towards professionalism, and who are often vilified for doing so, are right to be concerned. But how can rugby's administrators fulminate when it is the administrators themselves who have created this situation?

It is clear that in some countries, and South Africa is one of them, success is measured by results on the international field. How that success is achieved is not a prime concern, just so long as it is achieved. Everything that can be done to get the best players, to make them better and to make their lives easier, is done. The competition is fierce, the marketplace is full of other sports vying for television exposure, all of them seeking their share of the sponsorship and advertising cake. Countries in the southern hemisphere, threatened by the encroachment of rugby league and other football codes, have lived closer to the edge in this respect than those in the north. This is why the impetus for change has come principally from New Zealand and Australia. The law changes, the relaxation of the amateur regulations and the concept of the World Cup, all originated in the Antipodes. There is a far greater awareness and appreciation among administrators in that part of the world of what the international game is about and where it is going than there is in this country.

There are a few worthy exceptions, but the majority of the fifty-seven members on the committee of the Rugby Football Union don't have a clue what is happening in the rugby world. That is hardly surprising, given that most of them have reached their positions on the committee as a result of long and devoted service at the most junior of levels. They have no conception of what it takes to compete in the First Division of the Courage League, and are blissfully unaware of the rampant commercialism of the Super

Ten. Very few of them understand the scale of England's achievement in reaching a World Cup final four years after their humiliating exit from the inaugural event. To appreciate the effort required is to make a start in understanding what today's game is all about. But few are interested and still fewer seem to care. After England's match against Wales in the 1994 Championship, Dean Richards was telling a senior committee man on the RFU that he had lost almost a week's wages by playing for his country that day. The man was genuinely astounded. The shocking thing is that it should have come as a surprise. The RFU alone stands out against the payment of allowances and compensation for matches played at home. Even among the more enlightened members, whilst the head recognises the need for change, the heart is still firmly rooted in the past.

Yet they cannot have it both ways. On the one hand rugby is awash with money. Early in 1994 the Four Home Unions concluded a deal worth £34 million for the domestic coverage of rugby, and in Twickenham and Murrayfield, the game has two of the finest sports stadia in the world. The game and the image it promotes have never been more popular with potential sponsors and advertisers. Rugby is a boom sport, on the crest of the wave, but blanket media coverage and mass public appeal, like success, can be fickle friends. A few years ago, snooker enjoyed a position of unchallenged popularity. Television couldn't get enough of it. It was the same with athletics, but nowadays it is harder for both sports to sell themselves. Rugby must guard against a similar slump in public interest. Generally speaking the standard of league rugby cannot withstand the close scrutiny of live television. And no one would pretend that the Five Nations Championship has provided compelling entertainment in recent seasons. Complacency, lack of foresight and a collective mistrust of change are rugby's biggest enemies. For the moment, however, the game can do no wrong with those who wish to support it.

The players have never been more sought after. For the most part they are a credit to their sport. They are seen by captains of industry and by advertisers as self-disciplined, articulate, clean-cut individuals, the sort who would never let the side down and with whom it is beneficial to be associated. The RFU are never slow to take advantage of that for their own ends, yet they still resent the idea that any of the financial pickings should be diverted into the players' pockets. The argument that the players are taking money away from the game is as nonsensical as the charge that the driving force behind the players' wish to be recompensed for their efforts is greed. The image of the rugby union player as a money-grabbing opportunist is one that has changed dramatically in the last couple of years. It is now appreciated that all he seeks is recognition for the time and commitment he makes to the game. It is also understood that leagues, cups and championships, all of which are sponsored to the hilt, sit uneasily with the concept of amateurism. It's often said, and with every justi-fication, that the game's best sponsors over the years have been those employers who keep paying the wage bills while the players are away on rugby duty. In today's stringent financial climate that cannot be allowed to continue. It is morally unjust. Yet the differences between the RFU and the England players are as wide as they have ever been.

We have battled with them every inch of the way, but for every forward step we take we are forced to retreat a couple of paces, although the amount at stake is a pittance compared with the sums involved in other parts of the world. Powerful and vocal senior elements within the RFU have consistently risen up against us, despite the fact that we have asked for nothing which is not allowable under the International Board regulations. As one of those involved in the negotiations between the players' company, Player Vision, our agents Parallel Media Group and the RFU, I am seen by many within the establishment as a radical and a champion of the cause to promote professionalism. Brian Moore and Will Carling are viewed with similar suspicion and distaste. But nothing could be further from the truth. Had I wanted to make a business out of my pastime I would have given my all to cricket, and the many charities with which I have been involved and to which I have donated my fees for speaking and the like would not have benefited. We know what is happening in other countries and we see how cynically the regulations are being manipulated in order to feather the players' nests. Of course we are frustrated and irritated by the RFU's continuing indifference and inactivity. But we are asking nothing more than our due under the regulations and equality with players from other countries, and in this, I believe, we have the support of 99.9 per cent of the rugby community.

The principal bone of contention revolves around the regulations concerning communication for reward. We can advertise, endorse or promote whatever we like, from health food to condoms, provided we do it in a pin-striped suit or clothing other than rugby kit. Anything deemed to be rugby-related is off limits. The distinction between activities which are rugby-related and non-rugby-related is quite absurd. The very fact that we are being used in the first place is because we have achieved a certain eminence in the game, and to that extent everything we do in the area of advertising or promotion is related to the sport. The RFU's attitude is all the more galling when we arrive at Twickenham for the game against Wales, open the match programme and see three Welshmen, dressed in their national kit, advertising a product. Other countries, following the IB regulations, allow their players to wear rugby kit for promotional purposes provided that a percentage of the fee is retained by the Union.

However well intentioned the RFU might be it is the blatant hypocrisy and the double standards worldwide which are so infuriating. There are fund-raising dinners for the Wallabies in Australia, an All Blacks club in New Zealand, and a 'millionaires' club in Italy. There was the president of the Orange Free State, in the presence of Danie Serfontein, a past president of the RFU, talking about 'our professional – er – semi-professional game'. He was addressing a gathering at Bloemfontein organised specifically to raise money for the province's top players.

The rugby authorities might have a stronger case if they eased the burden on the players by reducing the number of competitions and games which we play. Instead of that there has been an explosion of rugby activity in recent seasons. In the summer of 1994 it would have been possible to have watched an international match somewhere in the world almost every week. The approach of the World Cup in 1995 will, for the first time, bring a clash of loyalties between club and country in England. Unreasonably, it will be up to the players to have to make that choice. What is certain is that they cannot play a full league and cup programme stretching into April and remain at the required level of physical and mental sharpness to participate in the World Cup the following month. And if, as seems likely, the only countries to gain exemption from pre-qualifying for the World Cup in 1999 will be the four 1995 semi-finalists, then the fixture congestion will be horrific. That convenient but trite little phrase about it being a players' game is hogwash.

In the mad rush to make money to build bigger and better stadia from which to make still more money, the players have been the very

My last game for
Toulouse and Christophe
Deylaud, the French fly
half, bears the burden.

Cuckoo in the nest. I
manage to confuse
Perpignan by wearing
their shirt in the final of
the espoirs tournament,
and finally win
acceptance as an
honorary Toulousain.

Sweet revenge. After his misfortunes in Cardiff the previous season, Rory shows Ieuan Evans a clean pair of heels in the 1994 match at Twickenham.

Brain power. Cambridge don Mark Bailey appears to have the angles worked out for Wasps, with cerebral back up from his former university colleague Fran Clough.

There is no more thrilling sight in rugby than Jeremy Guscott in majestic flight. John Kirwan is happy enough to cling to his coat tails.

Support for the skipper. Will Carling at full throttle, and I try to keep up.

Another boatload of reprobates from the Old Country arrives in Sydney Harbour. England's representation on the 1989 Lion tour posing for 'The Most Contrived Photograph of the Century' competition.

A thistle between roses. Gavin Hastings, Rory and I endorse the act of union after the Lions had beaten New Zealand in the Second Test in Wellington.

The frustrations of more than a decade are released after England's first Grand Slam success since 1980. The excitement must have been too much for me.

Modesty in all things. Will Carling, Phil de Glanville and I display restraint and humility in our moment of victory over the All Blacks.

Craig Chalmers comes uncomfortably close to charging down the drop goal which put England into the World Cup final.

Next question please. Emily holds an impromptu press conference at Belton Woods before the World Cup final against Australia. Mum and Dad lend support.

Hands up who thinks Rob Andrew should be captain of England. Will Carling approves.

A game of two halves. Michael Lynagh and I meet up in Durban for a natter.

Brief Encounter. Jack Rowell and Dick Best share the same platform at a press briefing in South Africa. But six weeks after the tour Best was dismissed as national coach. Rowell intends to do it his way.

The old firm. Morris and Andrew, an enduring partnership based on mutual respect and trust.

My second try for England. It helps seal South Africa's fate in the First Test in Pretoria, and Jason Leonard solves the mystery of the missing Springbok full back.

least of the concerns. When I opted for rugby instead of cricket as my sporting priority I did so for a number of reasons. Enjoyment and friendship were top of the list. The opportunity to represent my country was not then a consideration but to have done so, to have travelled the world, to have spent so much time in the company of so many wonderful people, to have sampled so many of life's experiences, has been a privilege, an honour and an unsurpassing joy. What I did not choose, however, was the road that rugby has taken and has been speeding along for the last decade and more. That was the policy of the game's governing bodies and the responsibility for the consequences of those decision rests with them. They cannot embrace those elements which suit them and contemptuously dispense with those which do not. They are either in or they are out. As I see it, rugby's administrators in this country have a straight choice to make, and that is whether or not they wish to remain in the mainstream of the world game. If they do, then there is no alternative but to accept the idea of semi-professionalism.

For that to happen, a framework would need to be installed to support the game financially. The Courage leagues as they are structured at present could not sustain a professional game any more than could the Heineken leagues in Wales, the McEwans leagues in Scotland or the Irish leagues. A new competition would therefore have to be established. Whether this is provincially based or whether it takes the form of an Anglo-Welsh alliance or a European super-league along the lines I have suggested, I do not know. But there is no time to lose. South Africa, Australia and New Zealand could be out of sight within the next five years. They could be joined by Italy and perhaps by Argentina and Canada who are being wooed by the southern hemisphere countries to participate in the Super Ten.

I am very fortunate to be, along with professional businessmen like Brian Moore and Will Carling, among the last of a generation of players who, thanks to the acceptance, understanding and devotion of a long-suffering wife and the acceptance, understanding and generosity of a long-suffering employer, have just about succeeded in balancing the equation. But if I were to come into the game today as a twenty-two-year-old with the same career pyramid that confronted me in the mid eighties, I simply could not do it. If, as pathfinders through the commercial maze, we have in some small way helped to improve the lot of the next generation of players, then we will at least have achieved something from our struggle. The Run With the Ball scheme we began in 1991 and which ran backwards for the first couple of years, is at last beginning to bear fruit. In fairness to the RFU they are even starting to channel some revenue our way by hooking us up with their existing sponsors like Isostar, Courage and Cellnet, and the players' fund at the end of the 1994 season stood at a much healthier total of around £250,000. But lest anyone gets overheated, that amounts to little more than £6,000 a man – not exactly a king's ransom but it does represent progress. What we would now like to see is the dismantling of that divisive barrier between rugby- and non-rugby-related activities, and the freedom to make whatever we can from enterprises off the field. None of us has advocated that we should be paid for playing but there is a very clear distinction to be made between this and fair recompense for activities unconnected with playing the game.

Whether or not the cumbersome structure of the RFU committee is geared to the voracious appetites of commercialism I am not sure. The most important single appointment at headquarters, next to the secretary, should be a highly skilled commercial manager, and rather than launching Twickenham into the space age, the additional revenue should be used to create centres of excellence along similar lines to the establishments in Australia and South Africa. To watch the standard of play in the under-21 provincial games in South Africa was simultaneously a thrilling and terrifying experience. The levels of skill were breathtaking, and with the right guidance both on and off the field, these youngsters will secure South Africa's rugby future. In so doing they will also help to secure their own futures, which is a luxury not permitted so far to their counterparts in England. But our under-21s are England's future, as they are rugby's future. They cannot hope to compete against the best in the world unless they are given the same opportunities as the best in the world. That is the stark choice facing our administrators. It is certainly not one that I would like to make, but by the time that choice is made my playing days will be over, and I can reflect on my very good fortune at having played the game when I did.

CHAPTER 11

The Perfect Ten

I can see him still – a bundle of nervous energy, a tightly coiled spring – Phil Bennett, the most artful of all dodgers pirouetting past the All Blacks' flanker, Alastair Scown, and detonating one of the greatest tries ever scored. It was that unforgettable game between the Barbarians and the All Blacks in 1973, the year before I began playing rugby at Barnard Castle. Bennett was the player I imagined myself to be in my moments of wildest fantasy. He seemed to me to have the lot. So nimble and light-footed that he appeared to skim a couple of inches above the ground. He could dart like a fish and was just as slippery to catch. He could kick from the hand with unerring accuracy and for one so slight and slender there were few better cover tacklers pound for pound than Bennett. He was as close as they come to being the perfect number ten and, without ever knowing it, he was the biggest single influence in persuading me that fly half was the position I wanted to play. I remember seeing a photograph of him in a classic kicking pose on the Lions tour to South Africa in 1974, and I spent many hours in the field at home trying to imitate his technique.

There are few more complex positions to play than fly half. That is why it takes time and extreme patience to settle into the position. I have been very lucky in my career that others have given me so much of both to enable me to mature as a fly half. Many young players come quickly to the top but, just as quickly, plummet to the bottom. The position demands a mastery of the fundamental skills not required in any other part of the field. The fly half is the playmaker, American football's equivalent of the quarterback. He is given an overview of the game and has the power to shape the play. But to do so he needs to perform at a higher level than most the three basic skills: 1) catching and passing; 2) kicking; 3) tackling. The half backs must be able to execute all three from all positions on the field and in every situation. Centres and wings for the most part are required to perform 1 and 3 but pay too little heed in my opinion to kicking. It is very important as a means of adding variety to an attack and causing uncertainty in the opposition that centres should be proficient kickers from the hand. When Mark Ella was playing fly half for Australia he was one of the most breathtaking runners in the game. He was less effective as a kicker, but the Wallabies had a young man at inside centre called Michael Lynagh who could do Ella's kicking for him. The combination worked brilliantly. It is equally important in defence that wingers can kick safely and accurately to touch. It can be no coincidence that two of the most effective wings in the last fifteen years, Mike Slemen and David Campese, have also been accomplished full backs. I have recorded elsewhere in the book the occasion when Nigel Heslop's kick out of defence from the tightest of angles turned a game against Ireland. On such apparently small things can success in international rugby depend. The full back must, of course, be able to kick, tackle and, when he comes into the line in attack, to catch and pass, but tactically there is less pressure on him than there is on the fly half.

It is therefore a matter of temperament as much as anything else. As a shaper and controller of the team's destiny, the responsibility on the fly half is great. So is the pressure. As Frank Keating so graphically put it in his book on the great fly halves: 'Gunsmoke sears the eyes of even a half-decent fly half. He operates in the very cannon's mouth.' That requires boldness and confidence, both of which come from immaculately honed skills. To reach that level of perfection takes a lot of very hard work. Attitudes to training have changed dramatically in the last ten years. The slogging round the field which was once the overture to every training session, and was the most pointless of all exercises, has gone. Very few drills nowadays are conducted without a ball. It is impossible to ever get enough of the ball. It is the only way that players can feel completely comfortable in a game when they have the ball in their hands. And that applies to forwards as well as to backs. Not so long ago when the Rugby Football Union, as part of a coaching exercise, put isolated cameras on individual players, it was discovered that a certain prop forward, a member of the national squad who shall remain nameless in order to protect his reputation and his family, went through an entire game without touching the ball. Well, that is not strictly true. He did, on one occasion, collect the ball from a spectator before handing it on to the hooker to throw into the lineout, but not once during the match did he have the ball in his hands. Yet the modern forward has to be conversant with the running game.

Mind you, there are at least two tight-head props of my acquaintance who are clearly frustrated fly halves and who spend almost as much of their time waiting for the ball outside the scrum as they do inside it trying to win possession. Another phenomenon which never ceases to amaze and amuse me – and you can see it on training nights all round the country – is the goal-kicking prop. Drop kicks, place kicks, kicks from the hand, left-footed, right-footed. The first thing he does before training and very often the last thing he does before retiring to the bar, is to practise his kicking, even though he will never come close to putting boot to ball during an entire season. I only wish that backs would show the same enthusiasm for a skill which they do need to perfect.

There is not a fly half of true international quality who is not a proficient kicker of the ball. This is especially true in the modern game, although I imagine that it has always been the case. I was too young to see Barry John in his prime, but the image I have of him is of a mesmerising runner given time and space to weave his magic. I had listened to the tales of his legendary feats and of how he once contemptuously sat on the ball in the heat of combat against a New Zealand provincial side in 1971 and dared the opposition back row to get him. But it was his kicking from the hand which ultimately broke the All Blacks in the test series. As much as we would all like to run with the ball and make any number of searing breaks or to deliver the scoring pass for the wing in the corner, the facts of international life demand that a fly half is a kicker first, a runner and passer second. There is nothing more soul-destroying for a pack of forwards who have sweated blood to win possession to see profligate backs toss it away behind the gain line. Equally there is nothing more uplifting for the forwards than a sixty- or seventy-yard kick to turn frantic defence into promising attack.

Before a big match I try to visualise myself in different situations in different parts of the field. I will spend a long time practising kicks from those areas of the field where we plan to attack. The up and under aimed to land just outside the opposition twenty-two can be a lethal attacking ploy. Outside the comfort zone of his twenty-two, there is little protection for the fielder, no place for him to hide. A yard too long, however, and the advantage lies with the defender. He has time to make the mark, he can clear his lines and the initiative has been lost. In itself, one kick overhit by a yard may be an unconsidered trifle, but a few small mistakes can have a big influence on the outcome of a match. In the Second Test against the Springboks at Newlands in June 1994, both Paul Hull and I missed clearing kicks to touch early in the game. Had these kicks reached their intended destination they could have eased the pressure on our embattled forwards. The Springboks would then have had to work harder to reclaim the lost ground and the psychological impact on both sides would have been very different.

Like a full back, the fly half must be able to kick competently with both feet. At international level, one-sidedness will be quickly exposed, whether it is in kicking or passing. There are few more satisfying moments for a kicker than a clearance struck cleanly off the weaker wing. The minimum clearance for comfort nowadays is the halfway line. We are into the era of the long-ball game and the ability to carry play from inside the twenty-two to the halfway line provides sanctuary and protection from all but the most prodigiously long goal kickers.

The restart is another crucially important area of the game and, again, one to which not nearly enough attention is given. Against the All Blacks at Twickenham in 1993, England kicked off. Nigel Redman took the ball cleanly and the pack drove straight into the All Blacks' twenty-two. The effect on our morale was electrifying. It had an equally demoralising effect on the opposition, who never fully recovered from the shock. The most dangerous opponents from the restarts are the All Blacks and the most expert kicker-off in my experience was Grant Fox. He landed the ball with pinpoint precision on the spot where his forwards wanted it. And on those rare occasions when he strayed from the straight and narrow, the forwards redoubled their efforts to turn bad ball into good. It is impossible to work too hard on restarts and my advice is to practise them in conjunction with the forwards.

Kicking is a very precise art, a very individual act. During the actual kick, whether it be from the hand or off the ground, it is almost as if the kicker is temporarily removed from the body of the team. He is like a golfer preparing to play a shot. There are external influences, of course, like the strength of the wind and the state of the pitch, but the kicker operates independently from the other team members who, for those brief moments, can neither help nor hinder him in his actions. There are some skills that every player must be able to perform – running, catching, passing, tackling and ball retention are some of them – but kicking is a highly specialised art which almost half the team are seldom called upon to perform, although Dean Richards in his adopted role as an auxiliary full back is a gloriously eccentric exception. But if kicking is an individual skill, running is very much dependent on the collective attitude and strategy of the team.

When England decided to shift towards a more expansive game for the World Cup final against Australia, it was a team decision. It was the same when we played the First Test against South Africa in Pretoria in 1994. The decision was made on the basis of what we had seen in the provincial games leading up to the test and once again it was reached with the full approval of the team. It could not possibly work otherwise. If the fly half took it into his head to play a running game which was contrary to the team strategy there would be chaos. But if the team are mentally attuned to a certain pattern of play they are more likely to be physically prepared. There is a better chance of support in the right place at the right time, and a firmer resolve to run at the opposition and perhaps to take greater risks.

There is certainly much less margin for error in the modern game. The popular phrase nowadays is to 'get into the faces' of the opposition, which may be more basic than Frank Keating's 'cannon's mouth' but is nonetheless descriptive. There is so much tosh talked about flat alignment and taking the ball as close as possible to the opposition defence. A lot depends upon the quality of the possession and the attitude of the players. We are constantly told about the ability of the Australians to bother and bewitch defences with their flat running three-quarters. It is one of the great myths lingering from the days of the Ella brothers, Andrew Slack and Michael Hawker, when the Wallabies did indeed sail perilously close to the wind. But defence was much less fierce in those days, and they were fortunate in having a combination of midfield players exceptionally and uniquely well equipped to play that kind of game. Australian sides of today are much more conventional in their approach. They kick first, they kick second and only when the risks have been all but eliminated do they seek to run. When England beat the All Blacks at Twickenham and were roundly praised for the manner of their victory, our backs actually stood a couple of yards deeper in attack than normal in order to combat the All Blacks' defensive alignment.

The problem is to strike the right balance. It is just as easy to become stuck in a running mode as it is to be chained slavishly to a kicking game. I have been constantly criticised during my career for the latter. But in the vast majority of cases the type of game I have played has been determined by circumstances and by England's strategy. Following the disappointments and criticisms in the early part of my international career, I decided to take stock. At Cambridge I had played off the cuff and as the mood had taken me. I realised that I didn't have a clear enough understanding of the game and my part in it, and whilst this was a weakness which might not have been exposed in another position, I was never going to pass muster at the highest levels unless I could come to terms with my role as fly half. At Nottingham, Alan Davies had encouraged me to visualise how I should play the game, but he was only partially successful, and it wasn't until the 1988–89 season that the penny finally dropped. I was more mature as a person, more relaxed as a player. Les Cusworth became a role model for me. He was coming to the end of a career in which the shining promise of his club rugby had never been fulfilled on the international stage. This was largely due to the imposition of tactics to which he was singularly ill suited. But in the autumn of his career he took the eminently sensible view that he had nothing more to lose and to hell with it, he would play the game for England as he did for Leicester, on his terms. He relaxed and enjoyed. 'You are much too intense, Rob,' Cusworth told me. 'Much too serious. Let yourself go a little and have some fun.' He was right, of course, but it wasn't until the 1989 Lions tour to Australia, more than four years after my first cap, that I fully heeded his advice.

I realise that many equally talented players have never been given the opportunities and the chances which have been presented to me, and for that I am sincerely grateful to my various mentors, in particular Geoff Cooke. But the point is that fly half is a position like no other on the field and as such it requires the patience and appreciation of the selectors just as much as the application and understanding of the player himself. The perfect ten nowadays is a very different animal to the classical fly half of fifty years ago, when swing-away passing, sidesteps and body swerves were the vogue. But there are qualities of fly half play which have stood the test of time and which are as important today as they ever were.

Speed off the mark is one of them, burning acceleration another. I have never been blessed with blinding pace, although over fifteen yards I have been known to beat Will Carling, something he hotly disputes and refuses to discuss. Passing, despite the changes in techniques, remains a vital weapon in the fly half's armoury. If he is more often than not the master of a situation he must also be a servant to those around him and, wherever possible, put them in advantageous positions. In many ways one of the most difficult positions to play is centre three-quarter, where, through no fault of his own but more often through the ignorance or carelessness of his colleagues, a player can be made to look at best ordinary, at worst a complete fool. If a centre plays badly it is very often a poor reflection on the fly half who has failed to improve the options of those outside him.

Above all, however, a fly half must be temperamentally suited to the position. If he goes to pieces, the chances are that the team will also fall apart. How often have I longed for the self-confidence which oozes from Jeremy Guscott's every pore whenever he takes the field. It stems from the inextinguishable belief in one's own skills and is strong enough to withstand outrageous misfortune. It is the ability to erase even the most calamitous error from one's mind in the almost certain knowledge that sometime, somewhere along the line, there will be a touch of match-winning genius. The right temperament, therefore, is the first thing I want in my perfect ten.

There could have been no fiercer examination of a player's temperament than that monumental World Cup quarter-final at Lansdowne Road when Australia needed to score a try against Ireland to remain in the tournament. The Australians were the hottest of favourites not only with the bookies but with themselves. Yet Gordon Hamilton's try had put the Irish ahead at a crucial stage late in the game. Nick Farr-Jones, the Wallabies' captain, was injured and the captaincy had passed to Michael Lynagh. 'How long to go, ref?' Lynagh asked. 'Four minutes,' came the reply. The most the Australians could hope for would be to get back down into the Irish half and scramble a field goal which would tie the scores and take the game into extra time. But Lynagh had other ideas. 'We'll go for the try,' he instructed. And that is exactly what the Wallabies did, the winning score coming from Lynagh himself with seconds to spare. Lynagh has the perfect temperament for a fly half. Unflappable in a crisis, calm and composed when the battle is at its most intense, his mind remains clear and his judgement decisive.

There have been many great fly halves more overtly flash, but few more effective. So much of his best work often passes unnoticed. Lynagh may not have Ella's power to mesmerise opponents and he is not renowned as a breaker-down of defences, but back-row forwards ignore him at their peril. Give him the hint of a gap and he will take it. More than anything else, however, it is Lynagh's phenomenal consistency which puts him in a class above his rivals. Very seldom throughout his long and distinguished career has he allowed his standards to slip. I first played against him at Cambridge when he was a student touring with Queensland University. Even then, as a novice, he was the linchpin of the university side.

Few possess Lynagh's length and accuracy kicking from the hand. It cannot be chance that so many of his spiralling punts parallel with the touch-line bounce at right angles into touch. They are inspirational gems for his forwards. Seldom does he show emotion, just occasionally betraying annoyance if his own game falls from the high peaks of self-imposed excellence. In common with the finest practitioners from every sporting field, Lynagh has the time and space to perform his art. He is the most difficult opponent I have played against, certainly the most highly esteemed, and in the list of modern fly halves he is unquestionably ranked number one.

If Lynagh lacks anything, it is genuine pace, the kind of explosiveness off the mark which makes old men dewy-eyed at the memory of Cliff Morgan and Jack Kyle. It was Kyle's record as the world's most-capped fly half which I overtook in 1992 when I was in Toulouse. By remarkable coincidence Kyle's daughter was a student at Toulouse University at the time and he had come to visit her during that season. There we were, a few miles apart, in ignorance of each other's whereabouts and I, to my eternal shame, ignorant even of the great man's existence. But I would very much like to meet him. Acceleration and deception by change of pace are assets as priceless today as they were when Morgan and Kyle were kings in their domain, and of the modern fly halves, none has been more extravagantly blessed in this respect than Jonathan Davies.

Of all the defections from rugby union, Davies has been the most grievous loss to our game. If Phil Bennett, my so-close-to-perfect ten, lacked anything, it was the kind of strutting self-confidence that Davies took on to the field with him. A swaggering arrogance, not a fault, but a virtue for fly halves and one which I have so often wished I had. Davies won his first cap against England in Cardiff in 1985. I played opposite him that day and couldn't believe his self-assurance. I was then in my second season of international rugby but could never have summoned up the bold precocity of Davies's performance on that occasion. He scored a try, and every time he had the ball in his hands, danger threatened. I have never again felt the same sense of inevitability I experienced watching him score a try against Scotland at Cardiff, an almost exact replica of the one which Guscott scored for the Lions against Australia. Davies ran at the Scottish defence, which appeared to melt before him, and with the most delicately weighted grub kick past Derek White was through for the try. Unlike most fly halves in the modern game, Davies sought to run first rather than kick, and so brilliant was he that he could lacerate well-marshalled defences even from the set piece. South Africa's Hennie le Roux is in the same mould but, as yet, nothing like as menacing. It is a measure of Davies's talent that he has gone on to reach even greater heights in rugby league, where he has added to his vast range of skills by becoming one of the game's outstanding goal kickers. If ever there is a way back for the lost souls of rugby league, Davies is the first I would return to the fold.

I have the temperament for my bionic ten and I have the runner. Now I need the kicker. There have been two outstanding exponents of the kicking art during my international career. One is Naas Botha, the other Grant Fox. I consider Fox to be the ultimate kicking machine, certainly for the accuracy and consistency of his goal kicking. As I have discovered for myself, rugby in the hot, thin air and on the flint-hard surfaces of the South African veldt is very different from playing on a soaking Saturday at Sudbury. So many of Botha's astonishing feats of kicking have been achieved at altitude that it is difficult to judge how his talents would have translated to other parts of the rugby world and to different conditions. Through no fault of his own, Botha has been denied the opportunity to prove himself on the world stage. There is no denying that he has been much less effective in European conditions than at home, although even in the twilight of his rugby days, during the Springboks' tour of France and England in 1992, some of his tactical kicking was exquisite.

Few players have succeeded in arousing such strong and such contradictory emotions as Botha. You either idolise him as a rugby phenomenon or you despise him as a self-centred mediocrity whose only talent is to be able to kick a ball. That may be as much the fault of South Africa's isolation as of Botha's undoubted egotism. As I have said, no fly half who purports to be of genuine international class can get to the starting rails without a mulish kick and a bullish self-esteem. The South African had both and he could manoeuvre the ball through the air with uncanny accuracy, but Botha, the whole Botha and nothing but the Botha, would not approach perfection as a fly half. His passing was not up to it, neither was his tackling and there were doubts about his tactical command.

Grant Fox, on the other hand, was one of the most tactically astute players I have ever faced. Very rarely did Fox take a wrong option and his importance to his country, not simply in the realms of goal kicking, can best be gauged by the All Blacks' lamentable failure to replace him. There was one fleeting moment during our tumultuous victory over the All Blacks at Twickenham when I thanked God for his absence. We were in the lead with the game moving towards its final stages. The All Blacks were mounting a series of increasingly desperate attacks. We knew that they were very close to surrender and that if we could hold them out now they had neither the energy nor the will to come back. In one final, frantic surge they were awarded a penalty close to their right-hand touch-line, midway between our twenty-two and the ten-metre line. Thinking that they would either go for goal or attempt a high kick towards our posts, Tony Underwood had moved infield from his wing. Zinzan Brooke, as he did so often for Auckland and for the All Blacks when Fox was playing, took up a position alone and completely unmarked on the far left of the field. Had Fox been playing then, even without looking he would have kicked across field for Brooke to score the easiest of tries. They had worked the move countless times before but still opponents were lulled into the trap. Brooke's arm was raised and waving frantically in an attempt to attract attention. I saw him too late to give warning but, mercifully for us, none of his team-mates had seen him at all and the chance was lost. A penny for the thoughts of Fox, who was sitting, powerless to do anything, a spectator in the stand.

Fox's kicking technique lacked spontaneity. Self-taught, it was calculated with almost mathematical precision and practised relentlessly, and it was the most successful in rugby history. No other player has achieved such a high strike rate and few have landed the ball with such consistency on or through its intended target. It is easy for scoffers to claim that any fly half could look good behind an All Black pack, but that is grossly unfair to Fox. Some of the New Zealand packs in recent times have been empty shells by comparison with their predecessors and it has been Fox who has held the ship together. Fox had the enviable capacity to obliterate the rest of the world from his thoughts every time he took a kick. It was almost as if he was entering a sealed bubble, a kind of capsule where time stood still, and when the kick had been taken, he would emerge to rejoin his team. There can have been few more single-minded fly halves than Fox, but when the occasion demanded, he was nevertheless prepared to sacrifice his own best interests for the good of the team.

There are two other great pivots with whom I have had passing (or kicking) acquaintance: John Rutherford of Scotland, and Argentina's Hugo Porta. Inevitably, Porta has been likened to a matador, but for me, watching Porta in his pomp was like watching Seve Ballesteros: stylish, handsome and capable of producing moments of shimmering beauty. I played opposite him only once and that was at the end of his career when, in the selfless service of an impoverished Pumas side, he played at Twickenham. But even in the midst of that massacre there were signs of the master craftsman at work. Like Porta, John Rutherford was one of those players who looked every inch a fly half. He possessed a grace and litheness which was different to Porta's languid elegance but produced the same frisson among spectators. A natural and most beautifully balanced runner, Rutherford struggled in his early days as a kicker, but a thousand or more lunchtimes at Murrayfield in the company of Colin Telfer transformed him into the complete fly half. I remember sitting with him at the dinner following England's 33-6 annihilation in the Calcutta Cup match in 1986. I was then in my second season of international rugby and he, although none of us knew it at the time, was getting sadly close to the end of his playing career. He was a marvellous companion, the ideal antidote to despair, and he could not have been more encouraging. 'You've got a wee bit tae learn yet,' he said, 'and I'll be happy tae gie ye a few tips. But ye'll hae tae wait until I've finished playing!'

I have been trying to think of a way of sneaking a piece of my Super Ten. Over the years I have been told that I can't play behind a beaten pack, that I can't run and that I can't pass. But to my knowledge no one had ever criticised my tackling. So perhaps I could contribute something to the defensive qualities of this Helluvahalf. As holder of the world record number of drop goals in international rugby, I might also be brought on, *in extremis*, to drop the odd goal. So here he is. Temperament: MICHAEL LYNAGH; kicking: GRANT FOX; running: JONATHAN DAVIES; tackling (and dropping the winning goal in the fifth minute of injury time): ROB ANDREW. It may not be Dudley Moore's idea of the perfect ten, but Boleros to him.

CHAPTER 12

View From the Bridge

Those who can, captain; those who can't, coach. Coaches, like bankers and building society managers, are not the most popular of breeds. They have been blamed for just about everything that is perceived to be wrong with the game. They are the scourge of improvisation and spontaneity, they have eroded the confidence of the most naturally gifted players, they have removed the fun and the flair and, worst of all, they are completely indispensable. The coaching gurus are nothing more than tin gods preying on the insecurities and uncertainties of their charges. In the irresistible grind towards collectivism and organisational efficiency, the individual has been submerged and forgotten. And then, just when coaches felt that it was safe to emerge into the open, came the Graham Taylor documentary. As if coaching hadn't suffered enough. That compelling hour of television did for the art of coaching what *It's a Knockout* did for the royal family. Warts, carbuncles, forty-seven bleeps and all, the mystique of coaching was very nearly shattered. Instead of esoteric technical jargon which could spirit victory from defeat, there was the language of the gutter, the last desperate resort of a man who had nothing more to offer.

The problem is that for every good coach there are too many bad ones. The good coach, however, is as valuable to the team as any individual, and there is no partnership as important to the collective effort as the one between coach and captain. It was Winston Churchill who wrote that 'It is at once the safeguard and the glory of mankind that they are easy to lead and hard to drive.' It is therefore both the responsibility and the duty of the coach and captain to ensure that their players are willingly driven in the right direction. For all its tactical diversities and apparent complexities, I

137

have always believed rugby to be a simple game. There are those with their loose-leaf folders and their wall charts who would disagree. But very often they are looking for problems which don't exist, searching for tactical answers to which there are no questions. And so it is with captaincy. So much of it is common sense.

In any group of people there are very few who are natural leaders. Most are preoccupied in getting on with their own jobs rather than burdening themselves with the responsibility of looking after others. They are happy to be led. Indeed, there is an almost primal need for someone else to be at the helm and to pilot the ship. The first thing to know about captaincy is that different ships require very different piloting skills and techniques. Captaincy of a club is not the same as leading an international side. But there are general principles which can be applied to both. In my spells of captaincy with Wasps, London and twice at international level for England and the Lions, I have encouraged the involvement and participation of one or two trusted lieutenants, senior members of the side whose views I respect. That is not a weakness nor is it the sign of an indecisive mind, provided that democracy is never allowed to reach the stage of anarchy. There are always individuals with something to say who feel compelled to say it, yet who are looking for leadership from others. They have no clear idea of where they or the team are heading. That doesn't mean to say that their ideas are any the less worthy or valuable. But I remember at Nottingham, Simon Hodgkinson warning of the dangers of allowing too many people to have a say in tactical planning and strategical control. On the field the final decision must rest, and must be seen to rest, with the captain.

In this respect it is easier to lead a club than a country. The club is a family. The players train together twice or three times a week, they play in the same team at least once a week, they socialise in each other's company and they have a personal knowledge and understanding of each other's strengths, weaknesses and problems that goes far deeper than the surface relationships formed at international level. But even within the club environment, the team comprises individuals from a wide variety of backgrounds, or varying degrees of intelligence, and with different psychological characteristics. Unlike soccer, rugby players have to perform duties on the field of play which are as different mentally as they are physically. In soccer a full back, a striker and a winger are, at times, interchangeable. Each could do the other's job without too much difficulty. This is not the case in rugby, where a fly half would be blown to smithereens as a prop and a prop, for all Victor Ubogu's ambitions and beliefs to the contrary, would be a figure of fun at fly half. They share a common purpose but they are two very different types of people whose approach and attitude towards the game must necessarily be very different. A captain should be able to understand these differences and must be able to communicate as an equal with both forwards and backs. He must appreciate that while the backs may be throwing talcum powder at each other before a match, the forwards will be throwing bricks.

First and foremost, the captain must have the respect of both groups as a player, whether he leads by example, in the Peter Winterbottom, Finlay Calder and Gavin Hastings mould, or is of the more contemplative variety, like Will Carling. No one in my experience has paid more attention to detail than Carling, a devout disciple of England's new testament preached by Geoff Cooke. When he was first appointed as England's captain, Carling was twenty-two years old. He had neither the experience nor a reputation on which to rely. He therefore leant heavily in those early years on the counsel of his senior players, but before he could do that he had to win their respect.

Few have understood the difficulties which Carling has overcome in his years of captaincy and all too few have appreciated his achievement in leading England to the heights they have reached since he assumed the captaincy in 1988. Every time England take the field nowadays the expectation is that they will win, yet a few short years ago the hope was that they would not lose. Carling has played his full part in that most rapid of transformations. Sure, he has received the plaudits, basked in the glory and benefited from the full-frontal exposure of the voracious media which has turned him into one of the best-known and most recognised sportsmen in this country. But it has also been at considerable personal cost. As already mentioned, the criticism has at times been so intense and unrelenting that he seriously considered chucking it all in.

Carling has devoted a great deal of his life to captaining his country, and if he is more autocratic in his approach now than he was when he first took on the job, it is because he is more confident in his own position and prepared to follow his instincts. But he is ceaseless in his quest to get the best out of his players. He is constantly on the phone between squad sessions and before international matches, anxious for information about the players' moods and attitudes, and about any problems which might affect their performances. Knowing how players are going to react to different situations is an integral part of the captain's job. Dewi Morris and Brian Moore, both combative and fiery individuals, require very different handling to Rory Underwood and Dean Richards. Over the years Cooke began to relinquish an increasing amount of control to his captain. It started with the Friday sessions before match days and gradually extended into the decision-making process. This took courage on Cooke's part but it was also a measure of the trust and respect he had for his captain. It made sense too to delegate authority to the man who would have to make the decisions on the field.

Carling's critics will never forgive him for what they see as his failure to change England's tactics when the going began to get tough. They cite three games in particular – against Wales in 1989, the Grand Slam game at Murrayfield in 1990 and the World Cup final in 1991. I have dealt with the World Cup elsewhere and the straight response to the criticism of England's game plan that day is simply that our tactics came within a Farr-Jones fingernail of coming off, and were more likely to succeed than any other strategy. In 1989 and 1990, the England forwards lost control and allowed themselves to be hounded and harried to the point of distraction. On occasions such as these it is extremely difficult to make any tactical alterations, especially when that strategy depends upon forward control. Throughout the Cooke years, England's game has been based on the domination of the pack and its ability to provide quality possession. We have never been masters of improvisation nor have we indulged in the disorder and chaos so beloved by the Scots and the Irish. If our forwards are unable to restore order and regain the initiative, then there is a limited amount that the rest of us can do to remedy the situation. In his position at centre three-quarter, Carling must therefore rely heavily on his pack leader for advice.

This is in contrast to cricket, where the number of decisions and changes a captain can make during the course of a match and the devices he has available to him are almost limitless. He can change bowlers, switch ends, alter his field. He can focus the attention of eleven players and concentrate all their efforts on the task of getting one man out. Not only that, but as a good captain he will have the most detailed knowledge about the strengths and weaknesses of his intended victim. Short-pitched deliveries to Graeme Hick; a cordon of slips and gullies for David Gower; and a cardboard cut-out of Shane Warne for Robin Smith. The subtle shifts and balances in cricket can, if shrewdly applied, influence the result. A captain's decision can change the course of a game, which gives him a power and an authority unparalleled in other sports. If a rugby captain must, above all, be sure of his place as a player, the priority for a cricket captain is that he be a good captain, hence the choice of Mike Brearley at a time when there were many more talented top-order batsmen in England.

There are times of course in rugby when probable defeat can be turned into unlikely victory, but more often than not it is luck rather than tactical thinking which alters the course of events. In the Second Test against South Africa in June 1994 we were hanging on for dear life. We were being badly beaten up front and it could only be a matter of time before we went under. Yet going into the final quarter we were just three points behind and, for all their pressure and dominance, the Springboks were beginning to betray signs of irritation. A lucky bounce, a defensive error or an indiscretion under pressure and it could be them, not us, confronted by the spectre of defeat. Unfortunately it didn't work out that way and, on the day, justice was done.

It is because of the massive influence exerted by the forwards that the ideal position from which to captain a side is probably in the back row, where there is a close proximity to the main action but from where it is also possible to get the broader view. In all my time with England there has been only one captain who was a forward, and that was John Orwin, of whom the less said the better. Mike Harrison, the captain during the World Cup campaign in 1987, was very much a stopgap, and Nigel Melville's tenancy was grievously restricted by injury. Had he not been so bedevilled by misfortune I believe that he would have made a first-rate captain of England. He was well positioned at scrum half to take decisions, he was self-confident, tactically astute and had the ability as a player and the strength of character as a person to be able to impose his will on the other members of the team. But Melville's last game for England was in 1988, the season before Carling stepped into the spotlight.

In no other major sport in this country has someone remained at the helm for as long as Carling. Between 1988 and the Second Test against South Africa in 1994 he missed only one match, against the Romanians in his first season of captaincy. He has led England through the most successful period in their history and has, in my opinion, as clear an understanding of the game and its tactical requirements as any captain I have ever played under. A good example of that came in the game against France in Paris in 1990 when Denis Charvet was playing in the centre. He was one of the most dangerous runners in the game but not the stoutest of defenders. The French centres played left and right rather than inside and outside, and, depending upon where Charvet was standing, Carling stacked all his runners into the Frenchman's defensive channel, with the result that Charvet was a broken reed and in no state mentally or physically to cause us any pain. I have the highest respect and admiration for Carling as a player and as a person. It will be a long time before his achievements and his record as his country's captain are equalled, let alone surpassed.

Of the other captains who have impressed me, Dean Ryan has been an outstanding leader of Wasps. It is true that he has gained a reputation for having a volcanic temperament and the ability to self-destruct. But he pushes the button less frequently these days, and on England's tour to South Africa he skippered the midweek side with commendable maturity and responsibility. He is the ideal club captain in that he possesses a keen knowledge of the game and has the priceless ability to keep his players motivated through a long and punishing season. That is the most difficult of all tasks for the club captain. It is relatively easy to motivate an international side playing four matches over a period of two months. It is much more difficult to sustain interest and maintain momentum for eighteen games over eight months at club level. I recall an occasion when the Cambridge side were travelling to play Saracens at Southgate. It was midway through the second term, the Varsity Match was a distant memory and we had other things, like exams, on our minds. The game, to be honest, was a wretched inconvenience and the bus breaking down *en route* was a further distraction. We arrived a few minutes before the scheduled kickoff in no mood for playing rugby. As captain, Mark Bailey clearly felt that he had a duty to raise his troops from their lethargy, but there was nothing he could do to change the atmosphere. In his annoyance and frustration he got up and shoved his kit back into his bag. 'Okay, lads. If that's the way you want it, fine by me. You buggers can play them on your own. I'm off.' And with that he walked out of the door. The effect was startling. We couldn't believe that he was serious, but on the other hand we couldn't quite be sure. Suddenly we began to concentrate on the game and how we might have to play without our captain. A minute before kickoff, and no sign of Bailey. The referee called us out and still he hadn't turned up, but as we ran on to the pitch, he was waiting for us in the middle. Nice try, Bailes, shame about the result. We still lost!

The coach, like the captain, must be something of an amateur psychologist. He must be able to read the signs, to gauge the mood. This is where Jack Rowell is so skilful as a man-manager and where he has been so successful with Bath. There have been times when Rowell has said nothing to his players for an entire week. He has felt the mood to be right and has considered that anything he might do or say would be superfluous and even disruptive. There have been other occasions when he has read the riot act to his players, not all of whom have been able to take it. Rowell is a highly intelligent man, a master of the English language and a mischievous player on words. He has the capacity to destroy a reputation or an overinflated ego with a quip or even a look. But one thing you will never do with Rowell is to take him for granted. He is always one step ahead, constantly challenging his players both physically and mentally. The Bath connection was no guarantee of protection or special treatment for the England players in South Africa, and it is doubtful if Rowell was more openly critical of anyone on that tour than he was of Adedayo Adebayo. But his criticism had the desired effect.

It is for that reason that a coach must remain detached from his players. He cannot – must not – be one of the lads, for the very good reason that he will, at times, have hard and unpleasant decisions to make. Overfamiliarity, apart from breeding the contempt of the players, can also cloud a coach's judgement. His role should be a more paternal one, firm but fair, with the sensitivity to create a family atmosphere. This is what Rowell achieved at Bath and it is what Geoff Cooke did for England. The team which won successive Grand Slams and reached the final of the World Cup was bonded by friendship and shared experience, as a result of which the whole was often greater than the sum of the individual parts. There was confidence without complacency. Gone was the insecurity of the mid eighties when the only thing of which a player could be certain was the uncertainty of his international future. And yet, there was no room for relaxation of mind or body. Cooke liked to keep his players primed, always on their toes. Rowell is the same. After one of England's lamer performances against provincial opposition in South Africa, Rowell got the players together. He singled out Jason Leonard for special attention. 'I'm not sure, Jason, whether you are genuine or whether you are just a crafty Cockney gathering caps.' It was said with an air of flippancy but there was an underlying hardness in Rowell's voice. None of us could be certain whether or not he was serious, but Leonard could not afford to take the risk. He played magnificently in the First Test.

Cooke was frequently accused of showing blind and misplaced loyalty to a number of senior members of his squad, and perhaps, in hindsight, he did keep faith with the old guard for too long, but he never stopped testing his players. I remember our opening game in the Five Nations Championship of 1992, against the Scots at Murrayfield. We had won 25-7 but it had been a flat performance. In the fortnight before our next game, against Ireland, Cooke circulated a questionnaire which was designed to make all of us think about England's targets for that season and what part we as individuals had to play in achieving them. The last question concentrated the mind wonderfully. 'What is it that makes you still committed to play for England?' It was not a threat but it sowed a seed of doubt in the minds of the players. Just enough for us to go out and wallop Ireland 38-9. There was an element of that in South Africa under Rowell. No one, not even the Bath players, knew what he was going to do. It was Cooke's team he had inherited and, quite rightly, he took the view that if any player was going to lose his place, he should do it on the international field, not on the strength of one or two indifferent displays in the provincial games. But psychologically he had put pressure on the players. He was testing us and those who failed him would themselves be failed.

There are no more than a handful of outstanding coaches in the world and two of them are Australians, Bob Dwyer and Alan Jones. One is a democrat, the other an autocrat but both, in their very different ways, have been conspicuously successful. Jones is no longer actively involved in coaching rugby union but still feels betrayed by some of those players like Nick Farr-Jones and David Campese who broke through into the Australian side when he was national coach. Jones did things his own very distinctive way, a way that was often unconventional and occasionally bizarre. He became known as the Great Communicator, not only because of his job in radio broadcasting which, now and then, conflicted with his many other duties and interests, but because he was constantly in touch with his players, not so much as a seeker of wisdom, but in the search for information about them and what made them tick. In his own way he managed to create the family atmosphere so essential to a harmonious and successful international side. The wheels came off the Jones bandwagon after the 1987 World Cup but his record speaks for itself. Furthermore, he had given Australian rugby a status and its players a profile they had never previously enjoyed. His success was in combining the paramilitary hardness and precision of his training programmes with an innovative and nonconformist tactical approach. He may not have had the technical expertise of some coaches but he plotted and schemed at a higher level than most and, at his peak, he used the extraordinary force of his personality to convert even the most reluctant minds to his way of thinking.

Dwyer is a totally different character. Emotionally more restrained, more flexible in his approach, less bombastic and, ultimately, more successful. In many ways he is similar to Alan Davies, the Welsh coach, who was in charge of Nottingham when I was at the club. I also experienced his style with England B. He was an innovator, a meticulous planner and was constantly devising ways of getting the players to think for themselves. When the B squad met before matches he would pre-arrange the dinner table settings so that players from different clubs sat together. He would make certain that forwards and backs were mixed together and would then issue each table with a questionnaire about the forthcoming game. That way he encouraged immediate communication between the different groups and personalities, some of whom might not otherwise have addressed a word to each other from the moment the team assembled until the time, three days later, when they disappeared. Davies hated cliques.

Technically, Ian McGeechan was the best coach I have worked with. He was also the most sincere, a combination which ensured that he got his message across. The Scots have been fortunate in having coaches of the calibre of McGeechan and Jim Telfer in recent years. Both have achieved great things with limited resources. Telfer coached Scotland to a Grand Slam in 1984, McGeechan followed him six years later. McGeechan went on to coach a Lions side to victory in Australia, something which Telfer was unable to achieve with the 1983 Lions in New Zealand. Perhaps Telfer, who had a reputation for being an intensely serious motivator, derived most of his power and inspiration from his Scottishness and was therefore only capable of succeeding within the narrower confines of his own country, but McGeechan himself has never been slow to acknowledge the massive contribution Telfer made to the Grand Slam victory in 1990.

I owe a lot to McGeechan. It was when I fell under his influence on the Lions tour in 1989 that the different parts of my game, which had been pulling in opposite directions, began to slot into place. That tour was largely responsible for shaping my outlook on the game and I wasn't the only Englishman to benefit from McGeechan's teaching in Australia. So much so that when we went up to Murrayfield for the Grand Slam decider the following season we were greeted by a memorable newspaper headline – 'ENGLAND PREPARE TO MEET THEIR MAKER'. McGeechan had the rare gift of commanding everyone's attention whenever he spoke. He did so not by profanity or tantrum but by the soft sincerity of his words and by a technical grasp and tactical knowledge which were impossible to ignore. If at the end of it you didn't want to play for McGeechan then I very much doubt if you would have played for anyone. No one in my experience has ever worked more assiduously to produce the winning formula, spending hours on video watching, analysis and individual assessment. Despite his retirement as Scottish coach he still has much to offer the game at international level and it would not surprise me to see him back. I very much regret that my opportunities of working with him have been restricted to two Lions tours.

Even more do I regret missing out on the Pierre Villepreux experience. Rugby for Villepreux was a combination of pragmatism and romance but more heavily weighted towards the latter. It was a game of continuous movement in which forwards and backs performed the same skills at the same levels, no matter what the conditions. Marvellous in theory, and in Villepreux's case he achieved it in practice with his teams at Toulouse. It was an exhilarating adventure, a magical blend of fleetness of foot, sleight of hand, continuous support and Gallic improvisation. It was, in fact, an irresistible blend of all the things that the French do best. The tragedy for French rugby is that Villepreux has never been given the chance to test his enlightened ideas on the national side. His detractors argue that his theories are fanciful nonsense which could never translate to the international stage, but I'm not so sure. I have spoken with him on a number of occasions and have been fascinated by his preachings. I am also convinced that France would have been infinitely more successful if Villepreux had coached them, although there are signs that Pierre Berbizier, who has survived the vagaries of the French temperament and the unpredictability of the French Federation during his term as the national coach, is beginning to draw the correct responses from his team. Jean-Luc Sadourney's try in the Second Test against the All Blacks in July 1994 will go down as one of the finest ever scored. It was a rare gem, straight from the Villepreux textbook.

Berbizier, like Geoff Cooke, started from a long way back. He had to pick up the pieces of the Daniel Dubroca shambles and was immediately confronted by a programme of rebuilding. Cooke's journey began even further back and took him a good deal longer to complete. Reconstructing a team is one thing, restructuring an entire system is something else. The job he inherited from Mike Weston following the World Cup in 1987 was ill-defined, the structure of the game in England was nonexistent. Cooke was the consummate professional in his approach. He had the most organised mind of anyone I have encountered in rugby and with it a clear understanding of where he was going. Where he led, England followed, and no one can seriously argue that it has been a bad journey. It has not always been an easy one and for Cooke it has sometimes been extremely tortuous. There were those within the Rugby Football Union, fearful that he was accumulating too much power, who wanted nothing more than to be rid of him. He has been accused of taking defeat badly but what is wrong with that? Far better that than the careless indifference which accompanied England's litany of failure in the early and mid eighties.

There were times when he did make errors of judgement but no one is infallible, especially over a span of seven years. The dropping of Dean Richards from the World Cup final against Australia became something of a *cause célèbre* but in my view the decision was justified on the basis of Richards' form at that time. I am less certain about Cooke's decision to drop me after the defeat by Wales in Cardiff in 1993. I felt that I was wrongly identified as the main culprit for England's performance that day and was made the scapegoat for our loss. It may well have been that Cooke and his co-selectors were influenced by the running sore of the Andrew v Barnes debate which had opened up again in the aftermath of the defeat, but whatever the reason for the decision I believe it was the wrong one. But not even Solomon could have negotiated those seven years without blemish. The effort that Cooke put into England's resurrection from the depths to a position of eminence in the world game has been incalculable. It is perhaps the most fitting tribute to him that, as a result of his work, English rugby should never again find itself in the state of terminal decay it was entering when he took office. If, ultimately, his batteries ran down before his task was completed, it was not before he had fully recharged and revitalised England.

CHAPTER 13

A Dream Too Far

Geoff Cooke had a problem. England were about to attempt what no other side in history had achieved, a third successive Grand Slam. The question was whether he should soldier on with the Old Comtemptibles who had done the business for him in 1991 and again in 1992 or whether he should begin to introduce a number of new players. He had more to consider than this one campaign in isolation. There was a World Cup looming and there was an infernal new law to contend with. Good, bad or indifferent, we knew that it would very probably have an adverse effect on England's game, which had been built around ball retention in the mauls and scrummage power. Now we had the 'use it or lose it' syndrome foisted upon us by legislators apparently heedless of the devastating effect their decisions would have on the game. In concocting this law they comfortably surpassed all their previous efforts.

There were a number of players coming to the end of the road, among them Wade Dooley, Jeff Probyn, Mike Teague, Peter Winterbottom and Jon Webb. Even if they played through the season – and all of them had intimated that they would – none of them was likely to be around for the World Cup in 1995. Following Paul Ackford's retirement in 1991, the only player who had followed him into the grassy meadow was Rory Underwood, who had bade his farewells to us at the end of the 1992 season and had written a book on the strength of it. A number of us, however, remained unconvinced about his commitment to shopping with the family on Saturday afternoons and, sure enough, he was persuaded to re-pledge himself to Cooke and country.

It was an enticing package that season. Not only was there the prospect of a third Grand Slam, but in the autumn, England were

149

scheduled to play Canada at Wembley and, for the first time for twenty-three years, the Springboks at Twickenham. And at the end of the season there lay the ultimate challenge of a Lions tour to New Zealand. The Lions management team had already been chosen, and although it surprised nobody it offered further encouragement for the Englishmen. Cooke was appointed manager and Ian McGeechan, who had built his successful Lions side in Australia around England's players, would once again be coach. For the first time for two years Stuart Barnes was once again snapping at my heels, and this time it was for real. He had made it clear to England's management that he was prepared to commit himself fully to regaining his England place and had been brought back into the squad. The previous summer he had captained the B side in New Zealand and was on the bench for England's opening match of the season, against Canada.

There was another distraction which was to have serious repercussions for me later in the season. I was returning to England after my spell in France and discovered to my horror that the Rugby Football Union were insisting that I serve the 120-day registration period. This had been introduced in order to discourage players from changing clubs and to dissuade clubs from recruiting players midway through a season. Strictly in rugby terms it made sense to put the brakes on overambitious clubs poaching players and overambitious players offering their services to the highest bidders. But none of this was relevant in my case. I had gone to Toulouse for business reasons and it was for business reasons that I was returning to London. Moreover, I was going back to Wasps, the club I had belonged to since 1987 and had captained for two seasons. There was no question of impropriety, no skulduggery of any kind. Everything had been done by the book. Yet the RFU, in their blinkered inflexibility, refused to budge. They somehow managed to bring Nottingham into the equation. To this day I cannot fathom what bearing my membership of Nottingham had on the case. I had played for the club long before leagues had been established but with their twisted logic the panjandrums at Twickenham decreed that I must serve a three-month ban from first-team rugby with Wasps. Phone calls, letters, telexes, faxes and formal appeals were to no avail. The sole explanation for the RFU's crassness was that if they made an exception for me then the floodgates would open, but it was a preposterous decision and one that could have been very costly.

Before the game against Canada, however, I was, if you will pardon the expression, in full employment with Toulouse, playing regularly for their top side and greatly enjoying the experience. Walking out from the Wembley tunnel in the footsteps of so many footballing greats was another exquisite moment to savour. I thought back to my days with my brother Richard on the farm. How many times had I scored the winning goal in a Wembley final or given England victory in the last minute? And now I could add that most famous of sporting arenas to my list. The surface was magnificent, much better than Twickenham where the grass is often too long. I can never understand why this should be. Twickenham gets little use yet the surface seldom comes up to expectations. It certainly cannot compare with the pitches at Parc des Princes or Murrayfield and lags a long way behind the flat, true surfaces in South Africa.

England's failure to dominate the sturdy and robust Canadians and lift our play above the mediocre was annoying, but at this early stage in the season it hardly seemed a cause for genuine concern. There were long months of rugby stretching out in front of us and the last thing we wanted was to reach a peak in September. That evening the two teams drank a few beers together at the Roebuck pub in Richmond. Jeff Probyn and I were sitting with the Canadians' leviathan lock, Norm Hadley. Hadley was an engaging personality and a bright cookie. He was a marketing executive for the Japanese spirits company Suntory and was at that time working in Japan, but he wanted to sample life in London, so what could be more natural or obvious than to invite him to play for Wasps? Like me, Hadley would have to sit out his three-month registration period when he arrived at the club the following season, a period of inactivity which was to be prolonged by a broken leg.

The full impact of my ban had still not hit me when England faced South Africa in November. Although I wouldn't be able to play for the Wasps first team until the 7th of February, I was still eligible for London in the divisional matches. I was competitively tuned for the Springboks game, which England won 33-16, on the face of it a handsome victory but one which revealed the supreme physical strength of the South Africans and concealed a number of England's shortcomings. The tourists had led 16-11 at half time and it was only when England began to expose a few of their technical deficiencies and their lack of mobility and fitness that the Springboks buckled. Nevertheless it was a satisfying win, and now only the All Blacks stood between us and a clean sweep of the major rugby-playing countries.

The Divisional Championship that season was given additional spice on a personal level by the renewed challenge of Stuart Barnes. London went to Kingsholm for the title decider against the South-West, and although we lost a shade unfortunately, I was well pleased with my own game. I scored a try and generally had the better of the contest. There was no reason to feel under any pressure. England had won their two internationals in the build-up to the Five Nations Championship and my own game was in good order. It was clear by now that Cooke had decided to stick with the old guard, concluding that their experience would be crucial in securing what for every other side in history had been an unattainable third successive Grand Slam. But on the eve of the opening match, against France, his plans came unstuck when Wade Dooley was forced to withdraw. Martin Johnson, Leicester's promising but raw young lock, was plucked from the relative obscurity of his preparations with the A side, and before he had been properly introduced to his new team-mates was whisked away with the rest of the pack to Feltham for extra practice. For someone who was still trying to remember the line-out codes on his way out to the pitch, Johnson gave a remarkably mature display. A new star had been born and although he took no further part in the Championship there were more honours awaiting him before the season was out.

It was perhaps the most accurate measure of our improvement over the years that our one-point victory against France by 16-15 was considered by all of us, Johnson apart, to be almost wholly unsatisfactory. Our try was a fluke, Jon Webb's penalty rebounding from a post into Ian Hunter's arms. All things considered, we were extremely lucky to win. Those of us who played in that 1993 Championship have frequently talked about it and have tried to offer reasons for our failure to achieve the elusive prize. There is no doubt that one or two members of the pack were in terminal decline. The new laws played a part in this. England could no longer control the set piece as they had done under the old laws. They were therefore less able to dictate the pace of the play, which in turn led the selectors to abandon that rock of ages at number eight, Dean Richards, for the looser, more mobile Ben Clarke. Talented though

Clarke was, we badly missed Richards' strength in the maul and his overall control at the back of the scrum. He was the rallying point for so many England players in both attack and defence. There was also evidence to suggest that Cooke and Dick Best, who had been appointed assistant to McGeechan in New Zealand, were distracted by their additional responsibilities with the Lions. The same could be said for Will Carling, who had begun the season as a racing certainty to captain the Lions but who, by the end of it, was glad simply to be included in the party. And finally, there was the jolly old unpredictability of the Championship itself, where every match was like a cup tie and where reputation and form counted for little.

As always, luck played its part, and on the day England played Wales in Cardiff that luck was very definitely against us. We had the ludicrous situation of a French referee taking charge of his first international. He made two critical errors by disallowing Dewi Morris's try and by failing to penalise Wales close to their posts for a high tackle on Morris. On top of that, Webb hit a post with a penalty attempt and the Welsh plucked a try out of thin air when Emyr Lewis fly-hacked up field and Ieuan Evans caught Rory napping. So Fate had turned out to be a fickle friend after all. We had lost 10-9, only our second defeat in fourteen championship matches but with it had gone our cherished dream of the Grand Slam.

It was a wretched Sunday, and for me an even worse Monday. It was the phone call I had feared since the last occasion I had been dropped by England – which coincidentally had also followed a defeat by Wales in Cardiff. That time it was Mike Weston on the other end of the line. Now it was Cooke. It was pointless to talk to him then about a decision which was irrevocable. Nothing I could say would alter the fact that I had been dropped for the next match. It was a feeling I had frequently experienced as a batsman. The numbing finality of being dismissed and the wish that those few seconds of time could somehow be rewound to give you another chance. I felt extremely aggrieved nevertheless. I, along with Ian Hunter, had been made the scapegoat for what was a team failure. I had certainly been no worse than any other member of the side that day and nothing that Cooke told me on the phone was going to persuade me that the selectors were right to drop me. Cooke alluded to the fact that my enforced absence from first-team rugby had contributed to a certain lack of sharpness. It was true that the week before the English game I was playing for Wasps seconds against London Irish seconds on the back pitch at Sunbury, hardly the ideal preparation for an international and a situation which would never have been countenanced in other countries. After Cooke's phone call I indulged in a bout of self-pity and cursed the RFU for their intransigence.

None of this changed the fact that I was out and Barnes, after a wait of five years which had included spells of thumb-sucking and foot-stamping, was in for the game against Scotland at Twickenham. Incredibly, nine years after winning his first cap against Australia, it would be the first time that he would start a match in the Home Championship. This was one he finished in style. He made a number of lovely breaks, the most spectacular of which paved the way for Rory Underwood's try, one of three that England scored. With every flashing break I became more despondent. Not only was I not going to play for England again that season, but my Lions place was now in considerable jeopardy.

I tried to console myself with the fact that Barnes had only begun to weave his magic after Craig Chalmers had left the field with a broken arm, which had reduced Scotland's midfield to a disorganised rabble. But try telling that to the press, many of whom were ecstatic after the match and were self-righteously demanding to know why England had denied themselves the pleasure of Barnes's company for so long. They were soon to find out, but not before they had mischievously speculated that I was seeking a confrontation with Cooke. That was nonsense. I had known Geoff since my days as a student at Cambridge. He had picked me for county, division and country for nigh on ten years and if there was anything I wanted or needed to say to him then I had only to pick up the phone. Which was exactly what I did. We talked over my position, and although he confirmed that Barnes would be in the side for the final Championship game against Ireland, he encouraged me to keep thinking positively about the Lions tour. The injury to Chalmers was serious enough to prevent him from going to New Zealand, which was cruelly unfortunate for him but which kept the door open for me. The problem is that doors have a nasty habit of shutting faster than they open, and as I sat in the Lansdowne Road stand watching Eric Elwood tear England to pieces, my spirits sank. Elwood had played his first game for Ireland two weeks previously, against Wales in Cardiff, and it was a blinder. For England the Irish game was a dismal end to a season which had promised so much. But the portents for the match had not been good. Too many of the senior players were demob happy, and on the Thursday night, a good number of them had gone drinking together. It was a throwback to the bad old days when the game was almost incidental to the activities surrounding it.

The defeat in Dublin forced a hasty rethink amongst the Lions selectors, who were due to sit down the next day to pick the thirty players for the New Zealand tour. I had left Dublin early on the Sunday morning with John Elliott, who had given me some comfort on the taxi ride to the airport. 'I'm sure you'll be all right,' he had said soothingly in response to my anxious proddings. Elliott was not involved in the Lions selection but as a trusted lieutenant of Cooke's, I knew he would have a fair idea of the composition of the party.

Strange how often the most important telephone calls I have received in my life have come in the middle of a hectic day at the office. 'I've told you never to call me here unless it is really important.' I don't think those were the exact words I used to Sara when she interrupted a deal worth millions, although it's very probably what I was thinking. 'You're in the Lions team,' she announced. 'How do you know that?' I asked. She replied that she'd heard it on the radio. In order to confirm it from a second source I phoned my best man, Andy Davies, who spends most of his life glued to Ceefax, and sure enough, it was true. The other fly half was Barnes. Was no one to rid me of this meddlesome man? Eric Elwood's challenge had come too late and the Irish rose up in indignation at the selection of the party, which included only two Irishmen, Mick Galwey on the flank and Nick Popplewell at loose-head prop. Their ire had been fuelled by the fact that seven of the English pack outplayed at Lansdowne Road had been chosen, the one omission – and, ironically, the one most crucially missed by the Lions – being Jeff Probyn. Not for the first time, however, the Irish made up for their numerical disadvantage with their spirit. Both Galwey and Popplewell were magnificent tourists, Galwey having the dubious distinction of receiving a nationwide ban from all go-karting courses in New Zealand on the grounds of reckless driving.

If the high proportion of Englishmen in the side was a subject for the press to get their teeth into, the selectors were to some extent vindicated by the fact that seven Englishmen played in the test pack which beat the All Blacks in Wellington. Nevertheless the pre-tour judgement was that the Lions' forwards were too predictable, too old and too slow. It was a theme which the New Zealand press took up with relish and which continued even after the Lions had opened the tour with a couple of convincing and well-crafted wins against North Auckland and North Harbour. Two more wins, against the Maoris in a pulsating finish after being 20-0 down, and Canterbury, silenced the critics, albeit temporarily. Since our very first get-together, six weeks before departure, McGeechan had been ramming home the message of control at the breakdown. This was essential for survival against New Zealand opposition and especially important under the new laws. Once again McGeechan had proved himself to be technically flawless in his preparation of the side. He had seen how much better southern hemisphere countries had adapted to the new laws and had devised methods by which the Lions could thwart their opponents at the breakdown by the creation of what could only be described as a series of mini-scrums, which would in turn give birth to the mauls. Through them the forwards were able to establish a bridgehead and provide quick, clean possession for the backs. The result was that not only did the Lions win their opening games, none of which could be regarded as easy, but they did so with a stylish adventure which sent the New Zealanders scurrying into their think-tanks. It was noticeable after our fourth consecutive victory that the opposition were making deliberate efforts to prevent us from winning quick possession. And, with the help of a few obliging referees, they managed to do this with increasing efficiency. But at this early stage of the tour the greatest danger to the Lions came from the rivalry within the tour party, always a good sign, although most of us thought that Richard Webster, the Welsh open side, was carrying things a mite too far when he very nearly shot Peter Winterbottom's foot off. It happened during a clay pigeon shoot and Webster, unaware that there was still a cartridge in his gun, fired in Winterbottom's direction. With Galwey on the track and Webster on the range, we now had a couple of potential killers on the loose.

If Winterbottom was having his work cut out to keep Webster at bay, I wasn't altogether relaxed about the challenge Barnes was mounting at fly half. I had scored tries in the games against North Harbour and Canterbury but Barnes had also been playing well before we hit turbulence a week before the First Test. It was bad enough for the Lions to be cut to ribbons by Steve Bachop and Stu Forster, the Otago half backs, to concede five tries and to lose the match 37-24, but to lose Scott Hastings with a fractured cheekbone and to watch Martin Bayfield free-fall from ten feet on to his shoulder turned it into a disastrous afternoon. It wasn't much better in the next match against Southland on the Tuesday before the test. I was chosen as fly half, which, even to the most cockeyed of optimists, might not have seemed an encouraging omen for test selection. When my nose was smashed and I was replaced by Barnes, that seemed to be that. But Barnes's head was accidentally cut open in a collision with Robert Jones and he in turn had to go off. To this day I'm not sure whether I got into the test side because Barnes was unfit or on merit. But as no announcement was made about unavailability through injury, I am assuming it was the latter. Strictly speaking, with a broken nose I shouldn't have been playing either.

Crestfallen in Christchurch. That's how the Lions might have signed off their postcards home after our defeat in the First Test. It wasn't the shattering experience of the Lions' First Test defeat in Australia in 1989, but the knowledge that we could so easily have won was extremely galling. Brian Kinsey's refereeing hadn't helped. In the very first minutes he awarded a try to Frank Bunce which he was in no position to give. And then, horror of horrors, with seconds left, he wrongly interpreted Dean Richards' all-consuming tackle as an infringement and, from forty yards out, straight in front of the posts, Grant Fox kicked the winning goal. Once again we had given the All Blacks too much respect and had failed to recognise the all-too-transparent weaknesses in their game. For McGeechan, who had come so close to winning a test with his Scotland side in 1990, defeat of the All Blacks had become almost an obsession. He knew how vital it was to win that First Test. True, we could and should have played very much better and the chances were that we would give a more respectable account of ourselves in the next match, but it was also the case that the All Blacks would be a very different proposition in Wellington.

Changes would have to be made. The pack had lacked authority in Christchurch and they were no more convincing the following week against Auckland when the Lions went down again. All three front-row positions were changed for Wellington, with Jason Leonard switching from the loose head to the tight, Popplewell coming in at loose head and Brian Moore replacing Kenny Milne at hooker. There was also to be a rapid elevation for Martin Johnson, the replacement for Wade Dooley whose bereavement was the subject of one of the shabbiest episodes in Lions history. Dooley's father had died while we were at Invercargill, and Wade had gone home for the funeral. The New Zealand Rugby Union had made an extremely generous gesture to this great player by inviting him to rejoin the party if he so wished, despite the fact that they had given their agreement to a replacement for him. But the Four Home Unions refused to sanction Dooley's return on the grounds that it was infringing the tour regulations. If ever a touch of flexibility and compassion was required it was now, but by their insensitivity and obstinacy, the Four Home Unions caused outrage amongst the touring party and provoked a vitriolic response from Geoff Cooke. The sole beneficiary of this lamentable decision was young Johnson who, for the second time in a season, found himself rushed with indecent haste into an international match of massive importance.

It was obvious that defeat for the Lions in the Second Test would mean oblivion for the tour. The midweek side was experiencing a very serious malfunction and on the Tuesday before the test had all but surrendered to Hawkes Bay. It was an important game for one or two players who still had the prospect of winning a test place, among them Will Carling. For the first time in his rugby career Carling was experiencing real failure. He clearly was not enjoying New Zealand as a country nor was he completely in tune with its people. His game was suffering as a consequence and his faltering confidence had been dealt a further blow the previous Saturday at Eden Park when he had come on as replacement at full back for Gavin Hastings. Hard though he tried in the game against Hawkes Bay, and he tried harder than most, nothing would go right. After the game, Barnes, who was captain for the day, had some harsh words for his colleagues. He, like Carling, felt that they had let him down and had ruined his chances of test selection as a result. Carling for his part lost out to Scott Gibbs, whose form on the tour demanded test recognition.

The build-up to the game was the most bizarre that I can remember. If the Lions team to play in the match was ever formally announced then it certainly escaped my notice. The reason for the cloak-and-dagger secrecy was the hamstring injury to Gavin Hastings, whose captaincy, like his play, had been well-nigh faultless. Right up until the eleventh hour it wasn't certain whether he would be fit. He had, in fact, told McGeechan on the Friday that he wouldn't play. On top of that the Lions had been forced to endure a farcical training session on the Thursday. It had been the intention to conduct it in private but when we got to the ground there were about three hundred school kids on the touch-lines and, worse still, on the pitch, which was waterlogged. We trudged from one field to another but it was hopeless. The session was a total shambles, a complete write-off. Hastings did not appear for training that day and did virtually no work the following day at the public practice. The eagle-eyed scribes were filing more words than usual after the session, although none of them had got wind of Hastings' bombshell that he didn't consider himself fit to play.

It therefore came as a pleasant surprise to see him getting changed into his kit at Athletic Park an hour before kickoff. Our spirits had been lifted by the conditions, which were as near perfect as it is possible to get in the windiest of the world's cities. There was the lightest of breezes, a clear blue sky and an invitingly firm pitch. Yet within a few minutes of the kick off we were all thinking that Hastings should have been allowed to follow his own instincts. Facing into the sun but under no pressure he had fumbled a high kick from Fox, and Eroni Clarke scored under the posts. Fox converted and we were 7-0 down. Hastings then missed a couple of penalty chances as the Lions made huge efforts to get back into the match. But our confidence was growing, bolstered by our line-out jumpers, who could do no wrong. So badly were the All Blacks faring in this department that they resorted to a piece of gamesmanship which was shameless but, because it made not one whit of difference to the pattern of play or to the result, was harmless enough. The All Blacks' physiotherapist came on to the field, ostensibly to treat an injury, and handed a piece of paper to Sean Fitzpatrick, the captain. Fitzpatrick read it and immediately made straight for the lock forward, Mark Cooksley, who was playing in his first international and was clearly out of his depth. Minutes later, Cooksley went down with what was later diagnosed as a hamstring injury and was replaced by Ian Jones. If it was a genuine injury then it was one of the fastest-healing hamstrings in medical history, because Cooksley turned up on the bench the following Saturday for the Third Test and replaced Jones during the game, apparently fully recovered.

By the time Cooksley had departed, the Lions were ahead. Hastings, who had regained his composure, twice hit the mark with penalties and I had the rare satisfaction of dropping a goal with my left foot. We had also put in a scrummage of massive psychological importance on our own line. More than anything else this seemed to convince the All Blacks that it was not to be their day. It was most certainly not Fitzpatrick's day. His questioning of the referee's decisions, which was tantamount to intimidation, had begun early. By the second half it had become a running commentary. It was from his handling error that the Lions countered for Morris and Guscott to send Rory on a thrilling flight past John Kirwan and in at the corner.

The match reviews were extremely kind to me. I had been pleased with the control and precision of my tactical kicking but none of it would have been possible without the exertions of the pack and the unflagging energy of Morris at scrum half. From stem to stern our tackling had been magnificent, our tight forwards immovable, and our loose trio inspired, and the margin of victory by 20-7 was no more than we deserved. After the game I went up into the dilapidated old stand at Athletic Park to do a live radio interview with Cliff Morgan on BBC Radio. I was surrounded by hundreds of boisterously excited British supporters, the evening sun was setting and Morgan in his wonderfully Welsh way was waxing lyrical about the Lions' performance. We chatted about times past and present and it brought home to me the very special privilege we enjoy as international sportsmen. The occasion was made all the more memorable by the fact that my parents had flown out for the last two weeks of the tour, and I felt that whatever happened in the deciding test at Eden Park the following week, their journey had not been in vain. The only blot on our landscape that night was that it should have been a series victory we were celebrating, not just a test win.

Even then we sensed that our chance had gone. The All Blacks, fired to new heights by the fear of failure and the threat of demotion to the ranks, were a very different side in Auckland. Their changes in personnel were subtle, their play was anything but, and although we briefly held a lead we had no more chance of preserving it than the All Blacks had had in Wellington. But for the Englishmen in the party, there was at least the chance of swift revenge.

CHAPTER 14

Safaris It Goes

I remember John Rutherford's story of how, on the plane home from New Zealand, the Scottish members of the 1983 Lions tour, who had suffered the ultimate indignity of a whitewash, decided that the next season would be a memorable one for Scotland. And so it was. They achieved their first Grand Slam for fifty-nine years. It was with precisely the same confident determination that the English contingent approached the return match with the All Blacks in the November following the Lions tour. We knew that we had let slip a golden opportunity of beating New Zealand in the test series. Of the three tests, the only one they had dominated and had deserved to win was the last. There was no question that they were beatable, and had it not been for the phenomenal accuracy of Grant Fox's goal kicking and the general control he brought to the All Blacks' play, then the Lions would have won the series.

On this tour to England and Scotland, the All Blacks would be without Fox, who was unavailable for business reasons, an uncommon excuse in New Zealand where rugby is very definitely a business in itself. In fact Fox must have known that the end was in sight. Very wisely he decided to get out at the top with his reputation intact, and two weeks after the All Blacks returned home from the tour, he made his retirement official. Without their master tactician and points accumulator, it wasn't at all clear how the All Blacks would fare. We were curious to know what type of game they would play. The two fly halves they had chosen in the party were as dissimilar to Fox in style and in the range of their skills as it was possible to be. The tourists had no choice but to play more expansively than any of their predecessors for the very good reason that neither Steve Bachop, who made the early running for a test place, nor Marc Ellis, the eventual choice, was renowned as a tactical kicker. The onerous and unenviable burden of goal kicking fell on Matthew Cooper and so magnificently did he respond to the challenge that, for most of the tour, Fox was scarcely missed.

The All Blacks cut a swathe through the English divisions and laid waste to Scotland. It was exhilarating stuff, regrettably punctuated by moments of intemperance and sourness. I confess to being at a loss to understand why it is that whenever British sides tour overseas the home unions are happy to accept an itinerary which would make the labours of Hercules seem like Playschool, but for incoming tours are prepared to make all manner of concessions to their guests. The itinerary presented to the All Blacks was a case in point. For their opening match, the tourists were confronted by a London side totally unprepared for a contest of this importance, and, predictably, we were annihilated. I could just imagine the English alickadoos sitting down before the tour and thinking up all manner of mischievous schemes and devices to inconvenience the All Blacks before they hit upon the cunning ruse of route-marching them to Redruth to play the South-West – 'Hellfire Corner will sort them out.' What they failed to take into account was the fact that it was a darned sight more inconvenient for the South-West players to get to Redruth than it was for the tourists, and that the local side would have felt much closer to home in front of crowds at Bath, Bristol or Gloucester than they did in the remoteness of Redruth. It was another example of muddled thinking within the game's administration.

Redruth was the scene of an ugly incident which lingered unpleasantly until the end of the tour. If the injury to Phil de Glanville was not as obvious in its attempt to maim as the disfigurement caused to Jon Callard at Port Elizabeth the following summer, the horrific image it portrayed around the world and its effect on concerned mothers was equally shocking. It is an accepted part of rugby life against New Zealand sides that if, for whatever reason, you are caught on the wrong side of the ball, you expect to be forcibly removed. Few of us have a problem with that and in ninety per cent of cases, I consider it to be legitimate. Going forward, the ruck remains the cleanest and surest form of possession, and no country in the world does it better than New Zealand. But I cannot believe, and will not accept, that players going into a ruck lose all sense of direction and control to the extent that they have no idea where they are putting their feet. What made the de Glanville incident all the more worrying was the fact that it happened at a stationary ruck from which the ball was never going to be dislodged. In such circumstances the act of rucking can begin to look suspiciously like stamping. It had about it the disagreeable odour of malpractice, although there was an element of doubt which the All Blacks were quick to exploit.

There could be no doubt about Jamie Joseph's intentions towards Kyran Bracken at Twickenham. A youngster called belatedly into the England side for his first cap, Bracken was cynically trodden on with malice aforethought. The fact that he remained on the field and played his full part in England's historic win is a glowing tribute to his valour and rich promise. It became clear as the day of the match drew nearer that Dewi Morris was not going to recover from a flu virus. Bracken had distinguished himself the previous summer with the A side in Canada and then with the Under-21s in Australia where he had partnered Mike Catt in a memorable win over the Australians. We had practised together the week before the All Blacks match and I had been struck by his self-confidence. He had a smooth pass, not unlike Robert Jones's, and one with which I immediately felt comfortable. He is bountifully blessed with speed, strength and a good eye, and he can kick with both feet. His tendency to take too much on himself is a natural fault for such a gifted player and one that is easily remedied, but possibly as a result of his injury, which severely restricted his movement and seriously disrupted his season, Bracken contented himself in the All Blacks game with sticking to the basics.

Few wins have given me greater satisfaction than this one. Our pre-match assessment of the All Blacks was spot-on. It was one of Geoff Cooke's favourite sayings that the eighty minutes we were about to play would never be repeated – 'Be sure to make the most of them,' was always his advice. A few of the older heads in the team knew that this would be our last chance of beating the All Blacks at Twickenham. Even if the World Cup returned to our shores in 1999, we wouldn't be playing in it. For this game England had gone for size in the back row, with Rodber, Richards and Clarke chosen to oppose Joseph, Pene and Brooke, a formidable triumvirate despite the absence of Michael Jones who had missed the tour because of injury. Nigel Redman, whose consistency over the years had been matched by his persistence, was deservedly given the chance of playing in the second row in place of the injured Martin Bayfield, and it was his catch straight from the kickoff which set us alight.

Our game plan had been specifically targeted at what we considered to be the All Blacks' inflexibility and their reluctance to counter from positions deep in defence. We therefore kicked long and deep at every opportunity, from the hand and from restarts, certain in the knowledge that without Fox and, on the day, without Cooper, who had withdrawn on the morning of the match, they would be powerless to answer our fire. For the plan to succeed the forwards had to match the All Blacks, and Jon Callard, who was winning his first cap, would have to kick his goals. The forwards did their job to perfection and so did Callard. He had been badly unsettled on his two previous appearances against the tourists, playing for the South-West and England A, but on this of all days, when it really mattered, he rose to the occasion. He kicked four penalties and I dropped a goal. We even managed on occasion to put our runners into space. Even so, it took an inspired piece of covering from Victor Ubogu and an equally brilliant spot of touch-line detection by Stephen Hilditch to keep John Timu and the All Blacks out.

You have never beaten the All Blacks until the final whistle. They may stick by their rigid plays and, denied forward momentum and deprived of a target to hit, their patterns become increasingly predictable and easy to contain, but they never give up trying. We had experienced the backlash with the Lions in Wellington and now the All Blacks were coming at us again with renewed ferocity. But our defence refused to budge. The All Blacks were further handicapped by the failure of Jeff Wilson, by far the brightest of their young stars, who had been pressed into service as a goal kicker in Cooper's absence. The previous week at Murrayfield, when he had scored three tries on his début, international rugby must have seemed laughably easy. At Twickenham it was impossibly difficult.

It was the biggest scalp England had taken in my time with the national side. For Cooke and Carling it marked the high point of their partnership. Neither had enjoyed the Lions tour to New Zealand, Carling for the reasons I have already explained, Cooke for the fact that he had felt himself to be on the periphery, ordering buses and tackle bags for training rather than dictating match tactics, which was very much the preserve of Ian McGeechan. I formed the opinion then, and I have had no reason to alter my view since, that the seeds of doubt about Cooke's future in rugby were sown in his mind during that tour. From the very outset of his career in management Cooke wanted to be involved in all its aspects, which included coaching. When he brought in Roger Uttley, it was as his assistant. After Uttley came Dick Best and then, to ease the increasing administrative burden which was falling on him, Cooke appointed Mike Slemen to assist with the backs. Ironically, it was that appointment which significantly reduced the hands-on involvement Cooke had enjoyed with the team. It was the same in New Zealand, where there was a clearly defined line between administration and management, and neither Cooke nor McGeechan was expected to encroach on the other's territory. This was very evidently a source of disappointment and at times frustration to Cooke, and when he discovered that a similar situation had arisen within the England organisation, the time had come for him to bow out.

If the win over the All Blacks had rekindled the dying embers of Cooke's enthusiasm, it was, I believe, a temporary postponement of his irrevocable decision to resign. How to do it gracefully with minimum fuss and upset to the team would be the problem. The announcement, a few days before our Channel crossing to play France in Paris, was not, on the face of it, a masterpiece of timing. The previous week England had suffered an inglorious defeat against the Irish at Twickenham. This had followed a thoroughly unconvincing victory in the Calcutta Cup at Murrayfield where Jon Callard had kicked five penalties, the last of them in the closing seconds of the match when the Scots had been penalised for handling in the ruck. There was a wicked suggestion afterwards that the hand of Fate had been mine, an allegation I strongly refute!

The press post-mortems following the Irish match had taken little account of the relative inexperience of the England side. That season we had a new full back, a new scrum half, new combinations in the second and back rows, Victor Ubogu in his first full season at prop, and no Jeremy Guscott. Phil de Glanville, who had replaced him, was as steady and reliable as they come, but we badly missed Guscott, a player of world class. Any side would. In the middle of this Cooke dropped his bombshell. The immediate media response was that Cooke had finally succumbed to the pressure relentlessly applied by his many enemies within the Rugby Football Union. But this was no more true than the speculation that his decision had been precipitated by the Irish defeat. There was also a feverish hunt for a hidden agenda which revealed nothing, for the very good reason that there wasn't one. Cooke had chosen that precise time to make his announcement because, had it been delayed any longer, he would have felt obliged to take the squad into the World Cup fifteen months later. By resigning when he did, Cooke gave the RFU time to appoint a successor whose first task would be to manage the side in South Africa that summer. Cooke had had enough, and after seven years of total commitment, who could blame him?

He still had to steer England through two more games, against France in Paris and a rejuvenated Wales at Twickenham. The evening before we left for France, he confided to a group of us, 'I hope I finish better than I started.' His first two games as manager had, coincidentally, been against France and Wales, and England had lost both. For Paris, Cooke had returned to the comfort and security of some tried and tested old friends. Dewi Morris came back at scrum half, Redman was restored to the second row and after a brief dalliance with Neil Back on the open-side flank, Cooke reverted to a physically imposing back row. At full back David Pears replaced Callard, not the first player to hit the slippery slope from saint to sinner in the space of a few weeks.

In Callard's absence the goal-kicking duties were entrusted to me, which was both a challenge and a concern. When I was on song I could strike the ball as cleanly and as accurately as anyone. The trouble was that I doubted whether my level of consistency was high enough for international standards. I had heard Jon Webb and Stuart Barnes extolling the virtues of Dave Alred, a guru from the West Country who had successfully adapted the methods and techniques he had learned during his spell as a kicker in American football. Both Webb and Barnes had made spectacular progress as a result of Alred's tuition, and earlier that season, I had decided to seek his help. He stripped my kicking technique down to the basics and gradually began the process of rebuilding it. Kicking, as I have said, is a highly individual and specialised act, requiring individual and specialised teaching. Considering the importance placed on kicking, and how many games are won and lost by it, it is astonishing how few people there are capable of teaching it. It is even more perplexing to discover the attitude of the RFU's coaching staff towards someone like Alred. He has several times offered his services to England but has met with an indifference which is in marked contrast to the attitude of the Australians, who have been wooing him to assist in their preparations for the World Cup.

In the days before leaving for Paris I had a refresher course with Alred. He refocused my attention on the small details, the fine print which can so often make the difference between success and failure and which is so easy to forget. With six members of our pack playing at Parc des Princes for the first time, we might get few enough opportunities to score points, and I had the feeling that every one of them would have to count. From the very first kick, I sensed that this was going to be my day. I had that indescribably good feeling that I couldn't miss, the same, I imagine, as golfers have when they are in the middle of a hot streak on the greens. I kicked five penalties and a drop goal and England had won yet again in Paris, 18-14.

In the circumstances it was recklessly premature of the Welsh to talk of winning the Grand Slam at Twickenham. Their re-emergence from the charred remains of the previous few seasons was remarkable and a tribute to the coaching and motivational skills of Alan Davies, but his taunts about the poor quality of England's back play and his boast that the Welsh backs would cut loose, rebounded badly on him and his team. To win the championship outright we needed to beat Wales by a margin of sixteen points, and although we failed to reach that target, our victory was as comprehensive as any against them in recent years. We hadn't won the international championship, we had missed out on the chance of another Grand Slam, but we had at least bade farewell to Geoff Cooke in an appropriate manner and in the style to which we had become accustomed under his enlightened leadership. I sincerely hope that it will not be long before he returns to the game in some capacity. Men of his calibre are in critically short supply.

If Cooke's resignation had taken us by surprise, it was hardly a shock to learn that his successor was Jack Rowell. There was no other possible candidate for the job, and once he threw his hat into the ring, his appointment was a formality, although the power of his intellect and the force of his personality must scare the pants off some at HQ. No one knew Rowell better than Stuart Barnes. They had worked together at Bath for many years, and Rowell had never made any secret of his admiration and respect for his fly half, both as a player and as a captain. Was I once again under threat from Barnes, was Carling's position as captain in jeopardy? In the squad sessions before the South African tour Rowell kept a deliberately low profile, seeing everything, saying nothing.

The thirty-strong party contained few surprises and was, in almost every respect, the squad which Cooke would have selected. Not even the Bath players had the faintest idea what Rowell was planning to do. The only change he had made of any significance was to replace Mike Slemen with Les Cusworth, his assistant with the A side. Within six weeks of the tour finishing he had also dismissed Dick Best. He intended to combine the duties of manager and coach. The uncertainty surrounding my own international future was unsettling but it was something over which I had no control, and it was hardly new. I have become reasonably philosophical over the years. I have always endeavoured to give of my best and if that is not considered to be good enough, then so be it. From the little I knew of him, I was quite sure that Rowell would at least give me the chance to retain my position, and the rest would be up to me.

England were embarking on a momentous trip to a country where a minor miracle had been worked. The first free and fully democratic elections had been held just three weeks before our arrival and Nelson Mandela's installation as State President had been a most moving and historic occasion. There was every likelihood that we would have the opportunity of meeting him and the chance to see for ourselves the changes taking place in a country which for so long had been a political and sporting pariah. The feeling of euphoria amongst all sections of the community was encouraging for South Africa's future. There were pockets of resistance, notably in the Afrikaaner strongholds of Bloemfontein, Potchefstroom and Kimberley but these hardliners form an insignificant minority.

It was a major disappointment that no time could be found in the schedule for a private meeting with President Mandela. We were, after all, the first major international touring side to visit the country since the elections, and I am sure that he himself would have wished it. But even in the short time that it takes to shake a man's hand, it was possible to experience the power and dignity of this most charismatic of world leaders. Mandela's presence at a soccer international between South Africa and Zambia a few days before our arrival had coincided with the Republic's first ever win against their old rivals, and no doubt hoping that his attendance would inspire the Springboks to similar heights, the South African

Rugby Football Union had invited him to Pretoria for the First Test at Loftus Versfeld.

It was an unforgettable day. Here was the man incarcerated on Robben Island for twenty-seven years coming proudly and without bitterness into the heart of Afrikaanerdom as their leader. Every member of the England party wanted to meet him, a request which was granted. The line waiting to be introduced to him stretched from one end of the field to the other and for every player there were at least three photographers jostling and, at times, fighting for position. It was a farce which detracted from the dignity and importance of the occasion. Jack Rowell told the President that he was his wife's hero. 'Jack,' Mandela replied, 'you are my hero for bringing your side to South Africa.' Enough to reduce the biggest and strongest of men to tears. Rowell, a captain of industry whose look can wither at a distance of twenty paces, is just a big softie at heart.

Rowell went down well with the players, applying a firm hand and a light touch when necessary. The Bath connection proved no obstacle. He granted no special favours to his old charges nor did he attempt to ingratiate himself with his new ones. It was a happy ship and, despite the results, a good tour. The first ten days were spent at Durban, considered by some to be too soft an option for a team trying to acclimatise to unfamiliar conditions and preparing for two tests against the Springboks. It was the management's view, however, that coming at the end of a long and arduous domestic season, the relaxing atmosphere of Durban would be preferable to a spartan existence on the high veldt. Playing at altitude was going to be a major problem, and one that had been regularly discussed in team meetings prior to the tour. In view of that it should not perhaps have been too much of a surprise when, at our first training session in Durban, with the Indian Ocean crashing on to the shore a couple of hundred yards away, Victor Ubogu, clearly experiencing respiratory difficulties, gulped, 'Christ, this altitude training is killing me!'

Everywhere we went the welcome was warm and genuine. Nowhere was this more obvious than during our visits to the townships. At Port Elizabeth we conducted a coaching clinic for about two hundred black boys whose enthusiasm for the game was a joy to see. Many of them had turned up barefoot and without any kit, but they were all as keen as mustard. After the clinic, Dean Richards introduced the team members one by one. Polite handclapping turned into rapturous applause and hero-worship when the names of Victor Ubogu, Steve Ojomoh and Adedayo Adebayo were called out.

Our problems on that tour were all confined to the pitch. We were performing in unfamiliar conditions and playing a game of width and pace which was equally alien to us. Furthermore, the standard of refereeing ranged from unacceptable to shameful. The worst we encountered was in the penultimate match of the tour, against Eastern Province at Port Elizabeth. It was a calamitous match for us and seriously disrupted our plans for the Second Test at Newlands on the Saturday. Not only was Callard hideously and callously scarred, but Tim Rodber, one of the heroes of the Pretoria test, and playing in the midweek side after replacing Dean Ryan early in the game, was sent off. Rodber's overwrought response to his assailant had without doubt been provoked by everything that had been allowed to pass by an incompetent referee, and although few would argue with the decision to send him off, his frustration and fury were understandable.

Partly as a result of that experience, which badly affected him, and partly because of a debilitating stomach virus, Rodber in the Second Test was nothing like the force he had been in the First. We missed having him at his best just as much as we missed the experience and close-quarter strength of Dean Richards, but the truth is that we were beaten fair and square by a better side on the day. The Springboks were motivated to the point of recklessness and the changes they had made to the side after their defeat in Pretoria made a crucial difference to their scrummaging and line-out play. Not such a happy ending to the fairy story which had begun the week before at Loftus Versfeld.

Few outside the England party gave us much of a chance of beating the Springboks in the First Test. We had struggled to find any kind of rhythm during the tour, mainly as a result of the referees' failure to allow us to develop our play, but also because of our own inability to adapt to the conditions and the style of game imposed on us by our opponents. One slender victory over Western Transvaal, the weakest of the provincial opposition, was all that we had been able to muster, although the midweek side had displayed encouraging signs of life in losing narrowly to South Africa A. We had also shown some improvement in our loss to Transvaal, who had nevertheless given us a lesson in the art of counterattack. Once I sent what I thought was the perfect kick into the corner about five metres from the Transvaal line. There seemed no choice for them other than to kick into touch but before we knew it, they were running the ball back at us, forcing us into last-ditch defence.

We had therefore decided to make a few tactical alterations for the First Test. Wherever possible we would carry the game to the Springboks, ball in hand. We would also take as much advantage as we could extract from the ring-rustiness of our opponents. It was their first international of the season, and with so many players to choose from, they appeared to have fallen between several stools. François Pienaar, their captain, wasn't fit and neither was the number eight Tiaan Strauss. They had selected a young, inexperienced loose head and were fielding a specialist loose head on the tight. And, on the evidence of what we had seen in the provincial games, they had no lock forwards of the dimensions of Martin Bayfield.

In the days leading up to the match I went to the ground to practise my kicking, which had been disappointingly erratic on the tour. The conditions at Loftus Versfeld are tailor-made for kickers. The surface is flat and firm but with just enough give in it. There was not a whiff of wind resistance and in practice the ball was flying for miles. On one day Naas Botha was at the ground. Botha is employed by Northern Transvaal as a fund manager, his job being to raise money for the players representing the province. On the day of the test, money raised from a number of selected hospitality marquees, which Botha reckoned would be in the region of £100,000, went straight to the players' fund. And still they talk of amateurism! On this occasion Botha was conducting a coaching clinic. We chatted about the conditions. 'You've nothing to fear from them,' he said. 'But it's a compact ground, the crowd will seem very close, and it's just a matter of keeping your nerve.' That was what was worrying me.

No matter if I was to keep playing from now until doomsday, I would never again experience anything to match England's opening twenty minutes in that game. All the things we tried, and a few of the things we did not, came off. Twenty-three points scored and only a quarter of the game gone. It was all over and the shouting had already subsided to stupefied silence. The try I scored was typical of our good fortune that day. Ball in hand, nowhere to turn, off balance and on my left foot. The ball could have gone anywhere, sideways, backwards, an air shot – who could tell? Instead it went rocketing towards the Springbok line, high enough for me to be underneath waiting for it when it came down. Unbelievably, Joubert, the Springboks' full back, had gone AWOL, and all I had to do was catch the ball and flop over for the try. At least this time, unlike my only previous try for England, I could claim to have carried the ball over the line.

There is probably nothing more infuriating for statisticians than those sporting types who claim to have no interest in scoring records. But in all honesty, I can say that I have never paid the slightest heed to my points-scoring achievements, and until I looked at the back of this book, I hadn't the foggiest how many I had scored for England. It therefore came as a surprise, albeit a pleasant one, to learn after the match that my twenty-seven points that day had established an English record for an individual in an international match. Of far greater importance and infinitely more satisfying had been England's win by 32-15 which ranked in value alongside our Grand Slams and the victory over the All Blacks at Twickenham.

To escape the clamour and congratulations of the after-match function, Dewi Morris and I found a quiet spot inside the ground. We were kindred spirits. We had been through the best and the worst of times together. We enjoyed that special relationship which had come from so many shared experiences. As we so often did before international matches, we had shared a room in Pretoria and that morning we had both felt the nerves pounding in the pit of our stomachs. 'Why the bloody hell do we keep putting ourselves through this?' Morris had asked. Now, in the solitude of Loftus Versfeld, in the moment of one of England's finest-ever triumphs, we knew why.

Rob Andrew's Career Statistics

(to 1 August, 1994)

Christopher Robert Andrew

Born: 18 February 1963, Richmond, Yorkshire

Educated: Barnard Castle School & St John's, Cambridge University

Clubs: Middlesbrough, Cambridge University, Nottingham, Gordon (NSW), Stade Toulousain (France), Wasps

Occupation: Chartered surveyor with DTZ Debenham Thorpe, London W1

Height: 5–9 (1.76m)   Weight: 12–8 (80kgs)

International record

Caps: England   59 (58 at fly half, one at full back v Fiji 1988)
        British Isles   5

Points: England   210   (2T 11C 42PG 17DG)
        British Isles   11   (1C 1PG 2DG)

Captain: England v Romania   1989
        British Lions v France   1989

International Record

1985

Clubs: Cambridge University & Middlesbrough

 5 Jan   Twickenham   Romania   (4PG 2DG)   Won   22–15

Clubs: Cambridge University & Nottingham

2 Feb	Twickenham	France	(2PG 1DG)	Drawn	9–9
16 Mar	Twickenham	Scotland	(2PG)	Won	10–7
30 Mar	Dublin	Ireland	(2PG)	Lost	10–13
20 Apr	Cardiff	Wales	(1C 2PG 1DG)	Lost	15–24

1985 International Championship

	P	W	D	L	F	A	Pts
Ireland	4	3	1	0	67	49	7
France	4	2	2	0	49	30	6
Wales	4	2	0	2	61	71	4
England	4	1	1	2	44	53	3
Scotland	4	0	0	4	46	64	0

Results: England 9 France 9; Scotland 15 Ireland 18; France 11 Scotland 3; Ireland 15 France 15; Scotland 21 Wales 25; England 10 Scotland 7; Wales 9 Ireland 21; Ireland 13 England 10; France 14 Wales 3; Wales 24 England 15

1986

Club: Nottingham

17 Jan	Twickenham	Wales	(6PG 1DG)	Won	21–18
15 Feb	Murrayfield	Scotland	(2PG)	Lost	6–33
1 Mar	Twickenham	Ireland	(3C 1PG)	Won	25–20
15 Mar	Paris	Ireland		Lost	10–29

1986 International Championship

	P	W	D	L	F	A	Pts
France	4	3	0	1	98	52	6
Scotland	4	3	0	1	76	54	6
Wales	4	2	0	2	74	21	4
England	4	2	0	2	62	100	4
Ireland	4	0	0	4	50	83	0

Results: England 21 Wales 18; Scotland 18 France 17; Wales 22 Scotland 15; France 29 Ireland 9; Scotland 33 England 6; Ireland 12 Wales 19;

England 25 Ireland 20; Wales 15 France 23; France 29 England 10; Ireland 9 Scotland 10

1987

Club: Wasps

7 Feb	Dublin	Ireland		Lost	0–17
21 Feb	Twickenham	France	(1DG)	Lost	15–19
7 Mar	Cardiff	Wales		Lost	12–19
30 May	Sydney (World Cup)	Japan (replacement)		Won	60–7
3 Jun	Sydney (World Cup)	USA		Won	34–6

1987 International Championship

	P	W	D	L	F	A	Pts
France	4	4	0	0	82	59	8
Ireland	4	2	0	2	57	46	4
Scotland	4	2	0	2	71	76	4
Wales	4	1	0	3	54	64	2
England	4	1	0	3	48	67	2

Results: Ireland 17 England 0; France 16 Wales 9; Scotland 16 Ireland 12; England 15 France 19; France 28 Scotland 22; Wales 19 England 12; Scotland 21 Wales 15; Ireland 13 France 19; England 21 Scotland 12; Wales 11 Ireland 15

1988

Club: Wasps

5 Mar	Murrayfield	Scotland	(1DG)	Won	9–6
19 Mar	Twickenham	Ireland	(3C)	Won	35–3
23 Apr	Dublin	Ireland (Milleneum)		Won	21–10
29 May	Brisbane	Australia		Lost	16–22
12 Jun	Sydney	Australia		Lost	8–28
17 Jun	Suva	Fiji		Won	25–12
5 Nov	Twickenham	Australia		Won	28–19

1988 International Championship

	P	W	D	L	F	A	Pts
Wales	4	3	0	1	57	42	6
France	4	3	0	1	57	47	6
England	4	2	0	2	56	30	4
Scotland	4	1	0	3	67	68	2
Ireland	4	1	0	3	40	90	2

Results: France 10 England 9; Ireland 22 Scotland 18; England 3 Wales 11; Scotland 23 France 12; France 25 Ireland 6; Wales 25 Scotland 20; Ireland 9 Wales 12; Scotland 6 England 9; Wales 9 France 10; England 35 Ireland 3

1989

Club: Wasps

4 Feb	Twickenham	Scotland	(2PG)	Drawn	12–12
18 Feb	Dublin	Ireland	(1C 2PG)	Won	16–3
4 Mar	Twickenham	France	(1PG)	Won	11–0
18 May	Cardiff	Wales	(2PG 1DG)	Lost	9–12
13 May	Bucharest	Romania	(1DG)	Won	58–3
4 Nov	Twickenham	Fiji	(1C)	Won	58–23

1989 International Championship

	P	W	D	L	F	A	Pts
France	4	3	0	1	76	47	6
England	4	2	1	1	48	27	5
Scotland	4	2	1	1	75	59	5
Ireland	4	1	0	3	64	92	2
Wales	4	1	0	3	44	82	2

Results: Scotland 23 Wales 7; Ireland 21 France 26; Wales 13 Ireland 19; England 12 Scotland 12; France 31 Wales 12; Ireland 3 England 16; England 11 France 0; Scotland 37 Ireland 21; France 19 Scotland 3; Wales 12 England 9

Rob Andrew's Career Statistics

1990

Club: Wasps

20 Jan	Twickenham	Ireland	Won	23–0
3 Feb	Paris	France	Won	26–7
17 Feb	Twickenham	Wales	Won	34–6
17 Mar	Murrayfield	Scotland	Lost	7–13
3 Nov	Twickenham	Argentina	Won	51–0

1990 International Championship

	P	W	D	L	F	A	Pts
Scotland	4	4	0	0	60	26	8
England	4	3	0	1	90	26	6
France	4	2	0	2	61	78	4
Ireland	4	1	0	3	36	75	2
Wales	4	0	0	4	42	84	0

Results: England 23 Ireland 0; Wales 19 France 29; France 7 England 26; Ireland 10 Scotland 13; England 34 Wales 6; Scotland 21 France 0; Wales 9 Scotland 13; France 31 Ireland 12; Scotland 13 England 7; Ireland 14 Wales 8

1991

Club: Wasps

19 Jan	Cardiff	Wales		Won	25–6
16 Feb	Twickenham	Scotland		Won	21–12
2 Mar	Dublin	Ireland		Won	16–7
16 Mar	Twickenham	France	(1DG)	Won	21–19
20 July	Suva	Fiji	(1T 2DG)	Won	28–12
27 July	Sydney	Australia		Lost	15–40
3 Oct	Twickenham (World Cup)	New Zealand		Lost	12–18
8 Oct	Twickenham (World Cup)	Italy		Won	36–6
11 Oct	Twickenham (World Cup)	USA		Won	37–9
19 Oct	Paris (World Cup)	France		Won	19–10
26 Oct	Murrayfield (World Cup)	Scotland	(1DG)	Won	9–6
2 Nov	Twickenham (World Cup) Final	Australia		Lost	6–12

1991 International Championship

	P	W	D	L	F	A	Pts
England	4	4	0	0	83	44	8
France	4	3	0	1	91	46	6
Scotland	4	2	0	2	81	73	4
Ireland	4	0	1	3	66	86	1
Wales	4	0	1	3	42	114	1

Results: France 15 Scotland 9; Wales 6 England 25; Scotland 32 Wales 12; Ireland 13 France 21; England 21 Scotland 12; Wales 21 Ireland 21; Ireland 7 England 16; France 36 Wales 3; England 21 France 19; Scotland 28 France 25.

1992

Club: Stade Toulousain

18 Jan	Murrayfield	Scotland	Won	25–7
1 Feb	Twickenham	Ireland	Won	38–9
15 Feb	Paris	France	Won	31–13
7 Mar	Twickenham	Wales	Won	24–0
17 Oct	Wembley	Canada	Won	26–13

Club: Wasps

14 Nov	Twickenham	South Africa	Won	33–16

1992 International Championship

	P	W	D	L	F	A	Pts
England	4	4	0	0	118	29	8
France	4	2	0	2	75	62	4
Scotland	4	2	0	2	47	56	4
Wales	4	2	0	2	40	63	4
Ireland	4	0	0	4	46	116	0

Results: Ireland 15 Wales 16; Scotland 7 England 25; England 38 Ireland 9; Wales 9 France 12; France 13 England 31; Ireland 10 Scotland 18; England 24 Wales 0; Scotland 10 France 6; Wales 15 Scotland 12; France 44 Ireland 12.

Rob Andrew's Career Statistics

1993

Club: Wasps

16 Jan	Twickenham	France		Won	16–15
7 Feb	Cardiff	Wales		Lost	9–10
27 Nov	Twickenham	New Zealand	(1DG)	Won	15–9

1993 International Championship

	P	W	D	L	F	A	Pts
France	4	3	0	1	73	35	6
Scotland	4	2	0	2	50	40	4
England	4	2	0	2	54	54	4
Ireland	4	2	0	2	45	53	4
Wales	4	1	0	3	34	73	2

Results: Scotland 16 Ireland 3; England 16 France 15; Wales 10 England 9; France 11 Scotland 3; Ireland 6 France 21; Scotland 20 Wales 0; Wales 14 Ireland 19; England 26 Scotland 12; Ireland 17 England 3; France 26 Wales 10

1994

Club: Wasps

5 Jan	Murrayfield	Scotland		Won	15–14
19 Feb	Twickenham	Ireland		Lost	12–13
5 Mar	Paris	France	(5PG 1DG)	Won	18–14
19 Mar	Twickenham	Wales	(1C 1PG)	Won	15–8
4 Jun	Pretoria	South Africa	(1T 1C 5PG 1DG)	Won	32–15
11 Jun	Cape Town	South Africa	(3PG)	Lost	9–27

1994 International Championship

	P	W	D	L	F	A	Pts
Wales	4	3	0	1	78	51	6
England	4	3	0	1	60	49	6
France	4	2	0	2	84	69	4
Ireland	4	1	1	2	49	70	3
Scotland	4	0	1	3	38	70	1

Results: Wales 29 Scotland 6; France 35 Ireland 15; Scotland 14 England

15; Wales 24 France 15; Ireland 15 Wales 17; France 14 England 18; Ireland 6 Scotland 6; England 12 Ireland 13; England 15 Wales 8; Scotland 12 France 20

BRITISH ISLES

1989

*Replaced Paul Dean (Ireland) on tour

8 Jul	Brisbane	Australia	(1C 1PG 1DG)	Won	19–12
15 Jul	Sydney	Australia		Won	19–18

1993

12 Jun	Christchurch	New Zealand		Lost	18–20
26 Jun	Wellington	New Zealand	(1DG)	Won	20–7
3 Jul	Auckland	New Zealand		Lost	13–30

WORLD RECORDS

The world's most capped fly half (58).

Most drop goals in senior international rugby (19).

Most points scored in an international between the major IRB countries (27 versus South Africa in Pretoria 1994).

Index